THE SYNAGOGUE AND ITS PEOPLE

DESIDER HOLISHER

ABELARD-SCHUMAN inc.

NEW YORK

Copyright 1955
by Desider Holisher

Library of Congress
Catalog Card Number: 55-6405

Printed in the
United States of America

Published simultaneously in Canada
by Nelson, Foster & Scott Ltd.

CONTENTS

One Almighty God. The Hebrew Bible. The Torah. A people of study. The influence of learned men. The prophetic teachers. The religious poetry. The first cycle of fifteen hundred years. The rise of the synagogue. The Talmud. The second cycle of fifteen centuries. American Israel.

The first Jewish congregation. The oldest synagogue building. Jews in Philadelphia. Colonial Charleston, Richmond, and Savannah. Early settlers in New Orleans.

The architecture of the synagogue. The multiformity of styles. The classic pattern. New designs. The humble prayer rooms. The process of growth. The interior of the synagogue. The traditional symbols. Modern symbolism. On battlefields and Army posts.

Social fellowship. Congregational celebrations. The enjoyment of companionship. Recreational events. Hospitality to the community. Visitors of other faiths. The sharing of the religious truth.

FOREWORD

The purpose of this book is to portray one of the world's oldest institutions, the Jewish house of religion as we behold it in the United States. As ancient as Judaism itself, the synagogue is the core of Jewish life, and its generating center. Throughout history the synagogue has exerted a lasting influence on man's knowledge, emotions, and impulses. In the midst of the dynamic currents in the present-day American environment, it is as much the nurturing force of Jewish existence as it has been in the past.

The religious and social practices of the Jewish people are rooted in the synagogue. In the course of time scores of independent yet related philanthropic, educational, fraternal, and good-will organizations have grown out of the synagogue. Nevertheless, its basic function has remained the same as it has always been. Concerned with man and the world around him, the synagogue's all-embracing interest expands in every direction, from the lofty thoughts of heavenly vision to the everyday life of the Jewish people. Through prayer and worship, instruction and study, social fellowship and community life, the synagogue gives expression to the spirit and the ideals of Judaism.

Under the democratic institutions in the United States, the Jewish community has developed into one of the great centers in Jewish history. Three centuries of steady progress have resulted in the establishment of about four thousand synagogues. Now, on the threshold of the fourth century, when doubts and fears assail the souls of many people, let us gain an insight into the contemporary synagogue and those who live with it and for it.

Abundantly rich and profoundly learned is the literature on the Jewish past and present. The intention of this book, however, is to draw a composite picture of the inner structure and workings of the synagogue by means of camera close-ups and narrative text. Through these media I endeavor to bring into focus the Jewish house of God as a human institution and to present its substance and its spirit. The graphic and verbal elements, inevitably restricted in space, blend together to unfold the inspiring story of the American synagogue in its most important aspects. The photographs displayed show type-examples of a cross-section of synagogues. They were chosen to illuminate history and to point up pertinent facts.

In the presentation of the subject emphasis is placed on the divine purpose of all synagogues in general, with no dividing lines. The synagogue is one and its people are one in the great House of Israel, though they may differ in their interpretation of religious principles.

I feel a deep sense of gratitude toward the many persons who have given me their gracious cooperation: the rabbis, the principals and teachers of religious schools, the officers, members, and children of the congregations. They provided me with valuable information, and endured discomfort with magnanimity while the photographs were taken.

Glancing back over the four decades that I have been observing the Jewish scene, the grievous events of the past years flash through my thoughts and bring to mind the thousands of synagogues that were the heartbeat of Jewry, in the countries of Europe. I knew a great many of them, spreading from the Atlantic to the Volga, and in the cities and villages clustered along the Danube. Some of them were signally famous, landmarks in Jewish history; together with the multitude of the humble and the unnamed, they were the exponents of the Jewish heritage for long centuries. During the passing of the ages great Jewish centers and their venerable monuments have succumbed to pagan destroyers, but the truth spread by the synagogue and tested for thousands of years has not perished.

In this volume the American synagogue rises as a living reality, linked through time to the continuity of the Jewish tradition. I shall feel that my efforts have not been in vain if I have contributed to a better understanding of it. I fervently hope that the book will be rewarding to many people. Jews who are familiar with the synagogue may derive pride and joy from it, and others may regard it as a compass pointing to the heritage that is theirs. It is my sincere wish that fellow-citizens of other creeds may also find it of value, for they will discover spiritual kinship with their own faith and similarities to their own religious home.

THE SYNAGOGUE
AND ITS PEOPLE

CHAPTER ONE

THE

HERITAGE

OF THE JEWS

"And ye shall be unto Me a kingdom of priests, and a holy nation."
(*Exodus* 19:6)

ABOUT thirty-three centuries ago, a people terminated four hundred years of slavery in Egypt, broke their shackles and started out toward their destiny. Many centuries elapsed—from the days of Abraham, when God put him to the supreme test of faith, until the emergence of Moses— before God entered into His covenant with the Hebrews. As they were streaming back into the land of their ancestors, at craggy Mount Sinai, God revealed to them through Moses that they would be unto Him a kingdom of priests and a holy nation charged with the mandate of spreading God's teachings to mankind.

A free and self-governing people, the Hebrews concerned themselves not only with their material affairs, but also with God's place in their midst. They established religious practices and instituted rules for the regulation of the individual and the community, which were basically different from those of other peoples.

The novel concept, Belief in the One God, took hold of and molded the young nation, imbuing its people with a new outlook on life and a new way of thinking. Both were in complete contrast to the beliefs and reasoning of the peoples who surrounded them. In the midst of warring nations worshipping many gods, engaging in cruel practices, enslaving and slaying their fellow men, the Hebrews believed in the One Almighty God who created all the world and ruled over the universe. Though not visible in body, they believed in His presence everywhere and at all times for He is God who is omnipotent and infinite.

The Hebrews found in God the Father of all men, Who, without exception, is equally accessible to every human being. The concepts of righteousness, mankind, man's natural rights, loving-kindness, and many other new ideas became known to the Hebrews. An organized living-together, governed by law and built on godly ideas, initiated with the Ten Commandments, animated the Hebrew community. The Law of God became current and stood above the new nation whose career had begun far back in the remote times of earliest antiquity.

The Most High taught Israel the great laws of life as they are recorded and unfolded in the Hebrew Bible which is the product of the particular genius of ancient Israel. Written by Jews over a period of several hundred years and almost complete about two centuries before the common era, the Hebrew Bible reveals the very essence of Judaism. In Jewish tradition, the Torah, or Pentateuch, the first part of the Hebrew Bible, the Book of the Prophets, the second part, and the Book of Writings, the third part, are most highly prized. Monumental in scale and profound in spirit, the Hebrew Bible is the foremost source of Judaism. Dealing with the manifold spheres of life, it is instructive in purpose and practical in scope. Jews cherish the teachings of their Bible as the key to happiness and to useful living, to individual and collective salvation.

The Hebrews were the first to have a Book of Law with a character of its own. It was not a legal code in our contemporary sense. It was much more: a Book of Teachings comprising the law of life, the commandments and the ordinances for Jewish living, the knowledge of God's will relating to duties the people owe to God and to the community of men. In this book, known as the Torah, the divine obligations and the human obligations of the Jews are set forth in a majestic text descriptive of human history and divine aspirations, religious rites and social ideals, legal rules and advice for wise living, all in all affording guidance and direction for man's life. The Torah, or the Book of Law, embodying the basic principles of the Jewish faith, lays the foundation of Judaism. It discloses a way of living that is animated by acts and deeds, bringing order and purpose into human life. The Torah holds first place among the sacred writings of the Jews: it is the first part of the Hebrew Bible.

Historically, the Torah fulfilled functions in ancient Israel, indispensable to the processes of an orderly society. Viewed against the background of that period, the Torah played, in part, a role similar to the public and civil law other nations instituted later. The Torah also contains religious and social beliefs which scholars of subsequent periods tried to build into systems of philosophy, dividing them into thoughts on theology, morals, and ethics. Ritual practices, too, are prescribed and described in the Torah, the mode of worship which brings man into communion with God. All these aspects combined in the Torah, or the Five Books of Moses, were designed to establish the pattern of life God decreed for the children of Israel.

A veritable manual on life, with religious, ethical, and social implications, the Torah was studied from childhood on. To gain all the knowledge contained in it, the people had to learn to read and to write. The rank and file of the nation, the rulers and the ruled, the peasants, the craftsmen, the laborers, and the merchants, were trained in the multifarious ideas deposited in the Torah. Thus illiteracy was banned, and the educational standard of the great masses raised. To be sure, the people did not always take to heart the teachings of the Torah, and they often sinned gravely against the Law. Nevertheless, the widespread education of the Israelites assured them the distinction of being a people of study and learning. And this they remained through the ages, for they were inseparably attached to the Torah and the Torah accompanied them down the long centuries.

Whatever events and situations of a personal or public nature occurred among the Jewish people, they were pondered and argued in the light of the Torah. Being the all-embracing Book of Knowledge and the common possession of all the people, it was publicly read, explained, and interpreted. In study groups composed of men with great knowledge and insight, the provisions of the Law and its meaning were discussed and commented on. The Torah inspired a round of literature, expanding into an accumulation

of numerous other basic writings. When Jews speak of the Torah, they think also of the many other books which had their source in the Five Books of Moses, written by and about divinely inspired men and women in ancient Israel.

Throughout Jewish history persons of eminent knowledge and intellectual endowment, possessed of the will to serve God and the people, have gained special attention in the Jewish community. Learned and pious men, teachers, poets, philosophers, and statesmen, responding to their inner calling, had a strong influence among the masses of Israel. Whoever they were, whether king or herdsman, however humble their origin, they were raised to eminence for no other reason than their spiritual contributions. The people looked with respect upon persons of knowledge, intelligence, and eloquence; such talents earned popularity and authority, the esteem of society. Ancient Israel produced a long line of personalities, who, under divine inspiration, came to the fore with superior spiritual achievements.

In the Bible Judaism has erected an eternal monument to a number of teachers and authors of various writings. A glowing spiritual world rises from the Sacred Scriptures of the Jews, a literature consisting of historical narratives, biographies, ritual and judicial essays, proverbs, and religious poetry. Taken together they radiate the glory of the Almighty and pronounce the will and the word of the Most High.

Great teachers and preachers in Israel are immortalized in the second part of the Hebrew Bible, in the Book of Prophets. Moved by their passion for the truth, the prophets have taught the essentials of the Jewish religion. They expounded the meaning of God's Law when it was misunderstood or misapplied. Towering personalities, drawn from all strata of the community, many of them rose out of obscurity from the masses. Interpreting the teachings of the Law, they made the people know and grasp the true idea of God, His law of righteousness, justice, love, and charity. When the king or the priest was in error concerning God's will, when abuse and evil practices violated the Law, the prophets repudiated the mighty and the powerful. Some of them, seeing that most of the Israelites had false ideas about their religion, gathered their courage and turned even on the great masses, lashing their consciences that they might mend their ways. If some of them preached decay and gloom, all of them saw hope in the goodness of God and in man's ability to repent and to have faith in the future.

The prophets surveyed the age of which they were the children and reflected on the future. Those who looked forward expressed ideas about the future as God has planned it for Israel and the human race. Thus, standing firmly on the fundamental teachings of the Torah, they broadened man's knowledge of God. The prophetic teachers were God's instruments in emphasizing the eternal and the universal in the Hebrew religion, in exalting the One God and the immutable ethical laws He transmitted to Israel. The enduring impact of the prophetic teacher lies in their forceful pronouncements of righteousness and in their vision of God's kingdom to be established on earth. With the Messianic concept the Prophets of Israel formulated ideas and set ideals for the Jews and the rest of mankind to grow on and to improve with.

God and His truth thrilled the poets and singers of Israel as much as they fired the intellect of its learned men. Poets and composers gave expression to the sentiments that stirred them in a pageantry of lyric poems and songs. A poetry of haunting beauty illuminated the feelings and mirrored the emotions of ancient Israel. Touching every fiber of the human soul, it continues to reflect the faith and the religious spirit of Judaism.

Many beautiful poems were put to music and chanted as popular songs by the masses. Their number gradually increased, and some of them, known today as Psalms, found acceptance in the divine services at the Holy Temple in Jerusalem. One hundred and fifty of the most important of these inspiring poems were collected in the Book of Psalms and were then included in the Hebrew Bible.

With zest and feeling the Psalms convey in simple yet lofty language thoughts about the Almighty and man's close relationship with Him. The problems of life and the dependence of every human being on God are sung in them. The Psalms relate our existence to the giver of life, the judge of all men, and the master of the world. With great tenderness the psalmists glorify the Most High, His grace and work in nature and in history. Dealing with the yearnings of the common man, and of all men, these songs of faith help people to approach God with words of praise, supplication, repentance, and thanksgiving.

The uniqueness of the Psalms lies in their directness and earthbound quality. They entered the Jewish prayer books and form a large part of the Jewish liturgy. The Psalms are recited and sung by countless people in churches everywhere all over the globe. These sublime pieces of religious poetry, composed by the lyricists of Israel, comfort and spur men and women of all nations and creeds. Through their universality the Psalms have acquired a permanent place and vital role in all houses of religion where the One God is worshipped.

About fifteen hundred years passed into history from the time when Moses, the great teacher of Israel, gave his people the Torah, to the time when the rulers of the Roman Empire reached out for Palestine and imposed Roman hegemony on the Jews. The centuries were eventful, indeed, for during that time the Jews lived through many phases of their existence, from the tribal beginning to an influential state with a distinctive culture of its own.

Neither the Hebrew Bible nor the Jewish religion enunciates formal articles of faith; however, they prescribe Jewish conduct and the Jewish way of living, which rest on eternally and universally valid principles.

Judaism put forth the roots for two other world religions, Christianity and Islam. Recipients of the Judaic spiritual concept which they interpret in their own way, both drew heavily on the Sacred Hebrew Scriptures. The Hebrew Bible is the time-honored legacy of the Jewish people, but its creative power and formative force are felt throughout the whole Western World where, known as the Old Testament, it ministers to hundreds of millions of non-Jews.

The spirit of God emanated from the Sacred Writings, and the worship of God made the people of ancient Israel conscious of His presence. Acts of worship are as old as the Jewish belief in God. The institution of prayer and common worship dates back to the Tabernacle of Moses and it continued in the practices at the Holy Temple. The temple King Solomon built in Jerusalem served as the center of worship for the whole nation. At least three times a year the people journeyed to the Temple for the great festivals and offered sacrifices. Glorifying the Almighty, they participated in the rich ceremonies led by the priests and enhanced by choirs; they recited prayers and sang devotional hymns to the music of harps, trumpets, lutes and other instruments.

With the destruction of the First Holy Temple the Jews were deprived of their central shrine of worship, and owing to this national calamity, local assemblies for prayer and study were set up. In the towns and villages where Jews lived, this new institution sprang up and became permanent in Jewish life. Many of these meeting houses were established among the exiled Jews in Babylonia, and among the Jewish population within the borders of Palestine. Thus, about twenty-five centuries ago, the synagogue came into being to live as Israel's unique contribution to world civilization, in addition to Judaism, mankind's oldest monotheistic religion. In the annals of history the synagogue is credited with having been the first type of school, which taught the Jews their religion and to pray in common worship as well. In time, the synagogue became the pattern and stimulative example for church and mosque.

After the erection of the Second Holy Temple, numerous local synagogues functioned side by side with the chief sanctuary in Jerusalem. This new phenomenon gave a new turn to Jewish life. Each synagogue was an independent establishment of the people, a popular creation to satisfy the needs of the masses. The synagogue had no privileges to offer to any social group, to state officials, or to members of a priesthood. It possessed the features of a democratically organized unit, grounded in the common people. Every person was considered equal before God and in the synagogue. Practices developed there which furthered the democratic community spirit among the Jews. Regular worship, with scheduled prayer meetings and rituals, the study of the Law, and participation in communal endeavors have given substance to the synagogue. When the Second Holy Temple was destroyed by the Romans, the synagogue became the sole house of worship, the central institution wherever Jews resided, representing everything God meant to them.

The characteristic features of the synagogue included the public reading of the Torah during religious services, and the teaching of the Law by well-qualified persons. As the teachers of Judaism, the rabbis came to occupy an outstanding position in the nation. This they achieved through their particular knowledge of the Sacred Writings and their ability to transmit the Law to the people. However scholarly the rabbis may have been, they did not discharge special priestly functions to make them different from, or superior to, the other members of the community. Judaism commits every Jew to holiness and priesthood, for the only priesthood it knows is that of service to God through holy living. Every adult may assume the function of leading in worship at the synagogue and teaching the people their faith. No lines of an ecclesiastical nature separate the rabbi from other Jews; the distinction is based on scholarship and teaching qualifications and not on any authority derived from any kind of special grace or power. Traditionally, Jewish laymen can and do perform religious acts which other religions consider as pastoral duties.

Reckoned in terms of learning and the spreading of Jewish knowledge, the rabbis in ancient Israel were the recognized arbiters in the Jewish community. In that time the marked division between the religious and secular phases of life, as we know it today, did not exist. The rabbis were confronted with the necessity of passing judgment on family, business, religious, and ritual matters, and searching the Law, they arrived at decisions accordingly. New and diverse situations and unforeseen problems were placed before them for solution, and new points in disputes called for answers. The written Law did not contain specific provisions for every case and all circumstances, and the rabbis, guided by their scholarship and wisdom, had to interpret the Law. Inevitably, a large volume of Oral Law developed from the many facets of practical everyday life, which complemented the Written Law.

Scholarship and wisdom have created a huge body of Jewish literature, known as the Talmud. In Jewish literature the Torah, or Teaching, represents the elder, and the Talmud, or Learning, the younger part of the Hebraic teachings and learnings. The Torah and the other sections of the Bible embody the primary, and the Talmud, the secondary source of Judaism. They have coexisted since the sixth century of the common era, and both constitute the religious and intellectual flowering of Jewish culture from which future generations have drawn spiritual nourishment.

In the course of the march of centuries, conditions of life and the environment in which the Jews lived have many times been altered greatly. The adaptation of the divine law to everyday needs in a changing scene continued for centuries. At first, expositions of and comments on the Written Law of the Torah were made orally and transmitted from generation to generation by word of mouth. By 200 C.E. the comments and decisions made by thousands of rabbis were written down and collected and systemized in the Mishnah, or the Text of the Oral Law. A remarkable product of scholarly effort, the Mishnah was the first legal code of Judaism, superseding the many previous legal compilations and attaining exclusive authority among the Jews. With the coming of new generations, however, this code, too, needed adjustment to new circumstances, and scholars and rabbis busied themselves with elaborations on and interpretations of the Mishnah. Their commentaries on it were compiled in the Gemarah. The Mishnah, the collection of all man-written laws, and the Gemarah, the definitive explanations and discussions of them, together constitute the Talmud.

Talmudic literature touches on a very large number of questions in a wide range of subjects. Applying keen logic in searching and penetrating methods of thinking, ideas on every aspect of life are represented in the Talmud. Included in its legal portions, called Halakah, are various branches of law, marriage, property, and criminal codes, and provisions for hygienic, dietary, and ritual life form a large body of statutes. In the non-legal portions of the Talmud, called Haggadah, we find maxims, parables, fables, legends, history, science, folklore, and imaginative preachings of rabbis and striking opinions of teachers. Filling numerous books with thousands of pages, a tremendous amount of knowledge is accumulated in this intellectual storehouse of grandiose dimensions.

The Talmud was in the making for about a thousand years. Both outstanding centers of Jewish learning, Palestine and Babylonia, brought forth their own Talmuds. Yet the Babylonian version was preferred by the Jewish communities outside Palestine, and along with the Bible it was destined to play a paramount role in Jewish history. It became a practical legal and moral guide, an encyclopedic textbook for the Jews. It was extremely influential in developing a cultural pattern during the centuries when the people of God groaned under the yoke of persecution. The Talmud carried practical knowledge and wisdom to the Jewish communities and proved a sustaining intellectual fountain, a strong cohesive power that preserved Jewish identity and unity when waves of fury and hate engulfed them.

As the result of deportations, colonial settlements, military drafts by their conquerors, and migrations caused by poverty, large Jewish communities came into existence in the East and in the West. Jews lived from Persia to Spain, in Arabia, all over the Roman Empire extending across the Mediterranean, in North Africa, the Balkans, and the Italian peninsula, with sprinklings in regions known today as France and Germany. Some historians, venturing to compile statistics, believe that in the fourth century substantial Jewish communities were established in more than three hundred towns and in many more agricultural settlements. They estimate the number of Jews at some four million within the Roman Empire and two to three million outside the Roman dominions. Jews participated in every field of social and occupational endeavor, except the pagan religious ceremonies practiced by the other peoples.

With the Jewish people forming minority groups among nations of different religions and cultures, Jewish history commenced the Era of Diaspora. A second cycle of fifteen hundred years passed, in which the fate of the Jews was interwoven with the streams of European history.

During the period of Moslem rule in Spain this country flourished, and developed a high culture. With occasional exceptions the state protected the life and the property of all citizens, and Jewish centers there attained great prosperity and influence. Writers, poets, and philosophers of this golden age in Jewish history left classics of Jewish literature; Jewish scientists, physicians, and astronomers, broadened with their researches the boundaries of knowledge in Europe. Their geographical studies and instruments were used by Columbus on his voyage to the Western Hemisphere.

In the twelfth century the Christian rulers drove the Moslems out of

Spain, and eventually they reigned over the whole of the Iberian peninsula. It was then that the Catholic clergy introduced methods of conversion by force. Instigated by the nobility and the clergy, violent mob terror swept through Spain in 1391 in which thousands of Jews were massacred and their properties plundered. The intensified persecution culminated in the Inquisition. A particular target of these cruel measures was the Marranos, the Damned, those Jews who had submitted to baptism, but who, with the flame of their fathers' faith in their hearts, secretly practiced Judaism. In 1492, after tens of thousands had lost their lives, the rulers of Spain vented the last dregs of their wrath on the remaining 300,000 Jews who refused to undergo baptism on pain of death. By royal decree they were expelled from Spain; all their possessions were confiscated for the benefit of the royal household; the synagogues were converted into churches; and the stones from the Jewish cemeteries were used for public buildings.

A destitute and homeless Spanish Jewry fled for safety to neighboring states. Groups of them found refuge in countries along the Mediterranean —North Africa, Asia Minor, the Balkans, Italy—as well as in France, Holland, and England. The descendants of these Jews, who later migrated to South and North America to become the first Jewish settlers in the New World, are known as the Sephardim, a term which denotes their Spanish origin, in distinction to their brethren in the faith, the Ashkenazim, who lived in Germany, and then all over North and East Europe.

In the early Middle Ages the Ashkenazic Jews were chiefly farmers though some of them were merchants, and they mingled freely and lived amicably with their neighbors. Later, however, land ownership became strictly forbidden to the Jews. They could no longer engage in agriculture and were driven into towns. Jewish sufferings reached a tragic peak during the numerous Crusades. On their way to the Holy Land bands of Crusaders attacked and plundered the Jews, and massacred them wherever they found them. From England, France, and Germany Jews were expelled, then recalled. Marked with the badge of the outcast, they were frequently protected by noble landowners against payments of a toleration tax, but they were likewise used as scapegoats for internal troubles. In these centuries of intellectual darkness and mass illiteracy anguish and uncertainty hung over the Jewish communities. The Jews were banished from cities and restricted to high-walled ghettos, which they could leave only during the day and where they lived on the edge of starvation. Excluded from artisans' guilds and forbidden to pursue any of the professions, they were compelled to earn their livelihood in small trade, peddling, and money lending.

From the sixteenth century onward new ideas began to flow through Europe. Struggling for religious reformation, Protestant Christianity rediscovered the Bible. Written in Latin and understood only by a very few, it was translated into the vernacular so that the great masses might get to know it. The Old Testament gained in importance, and some of the finest spirits among the Protestant scholars, who could read the Hebrew

Bible and the Talmud in original, came to the defense of the Jews and their literature.

The situation of the people of the synagogue improved only very slowly. The transformation of northern Europe, England, and parts of Bohemia and Hungary into Protestant countries wrought deep changes in Western civilization. The restrictions surrounding the Jewish communities continued, however, and Jewish mass migration turned toward Poland, and the central and eastern parts of Europe. Jews had lived there before, but from the time of the Crusades many more Jews found their way eastward, especially into Poland. The Jewish population increased by a stream of newcomers in Poland, and it grew large in size and wealthy in means. At first, these immigrants were welcomed, and their contributions as farmers, artisans, manufacturers, merchants, and public servants were greatly appreciated. Protection assured them self-government in their communities and freedom of education. Many synagogues and schools, and famous academies of learning headed by renowned Talmudic scholars were established, just as a long time ago in Babylonia and Spain, a highly developed Jewish culture evolved in the communities of Polish Jewry. In the turbulence of wars between contending nations, Polish Jewry was reduced and impoverished, and then thrown on the mercy of the czars.

Under the impact of the Enlightenment the walls of the ghettos crumbled. But though the legal barriers against the people of the synagogue had fallen, prejudice against them and discrimination were too deeply ingrained when they entered the national life of the countries of their birth. Delivered from the status of a suppressed people without any rights, the social and economic disabilities of the Jews persisted, and serious incidents of anti-Semitism flared up in several countries of Europe.

Measured by the broad span of Jewish history and in terms of the ethical teachings of Judaism, the Middle Ages actually did not end until the birth of the United States of America. A religion of human rights and cooperation, of individual freedom with strict moral laws for the subordination of the self to the common good, of practical rationalization to foster advancement and of universal brotherhood to ensure peace for mankind, Judaism has decisively contributed to the spiritual foundations of the American nation whose pattern of life is rooted in these principles.

Jews have brought with them to America a heritage combining principles of eternal validity, religious customs and rituals symbolic of God's immortal truth, and the historical experience of three thousand years. Bearing witness to their divine and human heritage, Jewish citizens form a religious fellowship which is bound together by a common faith and memories of a common past. As other religious groups, Jews have their own convictions and traditions. Opinions regarding forms and rites may separate them, attitudes toward timely questions may differ, and factions may argue for their particular points of view, but the underlying philosophy of Judaism is the strong bond that unites and identifies American Israel and leads it to religious solidarity and joint action. In its fundamentals

Judaism is a religion of democratic principles congenial with the principles prevailing in the larger American community. The aim and the purpose of the synagogue is to keep Judaism vital, and the people of the synagogue, by the very concept of their religion, are inevitably bound to build democracy for the fulfillment of a better tomorrow.

CHAPTER TWO

AMERICA'S
EARLY
CONGREGATIONS

"And let them make Me a sanctuary,
that I may dwell among them."
(*Exodus* 25:8)

The story of the Jewish community in America began three hundred years ago, and it was then that the first Jewish settlers established a congregation upon their arrival in New Amsterdam. Founded in 1654, Congregation Shearith Israel, "The Remnants of Israel," was destined to become a pioneer institution of American Jewry. This oldest Jewish congregation in the United States has served the community continuously from the time its members worshipped in private homes until our day when it occupies one of the imposing religious structures of New York City.

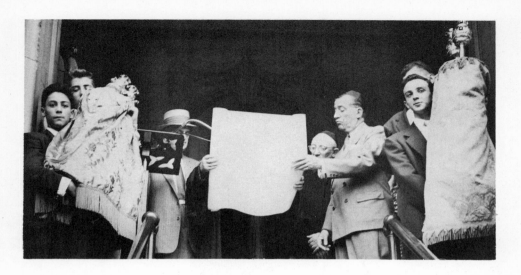

In 1954 a memorable event took place from the steps beneath the soaring columns of Shearith Israel. Flanked by two Torahs from colonial times, the American Jewish Tercentenary Committee proclaimed a nationwide celebration of the three hundredth anniversary of Jewish life in America. Signed by representatives of Orthodox, Conservative, and Reform rabbinic and synagogue bodies, the proclamation was read by rabbis in English, Hebrew, and Yiddish:

"By the grace of God and under the protection of the Constitution of the United States, we have lived and prospered in this land. We have been an integral part of American life. We have worked with all other Americans in the never-ending search for the democratic way of life and for the light of faith. Our ancient prophetic ideals and the teachings of the sages have been foundation stones of this nation. Our work, our hopes, and above all, our living religion, have been among our proudest offerings to the American community." Then it noted: "In some lands across the seas our brethren have felt the searing flame of prejudice, persecution and death. We in America have had the sad yet inspiring opportunity to save the lives of scores of thousands—to bring comfort to the oppressed, to help in the making of a new and honored nation on the ancient soil of Israel . . ."

The proclamation went on to declare: "But within the home of America we have succeeded in preserving the unique identity of the Jewish religion, worshipping in keeping with our historic tradition; and we have preserved our ancient teachings, our ethics, and our religious ideals in the free climate of our nation. Our religion is strong, as our American loyalty is strong." The conclusion of the proclamation summoned the five million American Jews to celebrate the tercentenary with thanksgiving, prayer, and study: "We call on all our brethren throughout the nation to offer thanks unto the Lord for the blessings bestowed on us in America; to pray for the continued peace and prosperity of our country and all its inhabitants and to rededicate ourselves to the ideals of our faith within the freedom of American democracy."

Along with other settlers Jews landed on the shores of North America at an early date when the clearing of the wilderness had begun. Among the first colonists was a group of twenty-three Jews, who had sailed from Brazil and arrived in New Amsterdam in September, 1654. Having fled from the menace of persecution in Brazil, they, like the Pilgrims and the Puritans a few years before in New England, arrived on this continent in search of freedom and peace. Following an arduous struggle with the hostile Governor Stuyvesant, the Jewish pilgrims succeeded in acquiring citizenship rights and in purchasing a small burial plot. But it was not until seventy-five years later that the Jewish community was able to erect a permanent synagogue building. Until then it had worshipped in rented rooms.

The first synagogue in the United States, the famous Mill Street Synagogue, located in New York's lower Manhattan, was dedicated in 1730, and some of its ceremonial objects are still in possession of Shearith Israel. The congregation has also preserved, carefully guarded in its archives, many of its original documents and minute books, which throw light on the story of the Jewish pioneers in America. Through scholarly devotion and meticulous research, based on records, membership rolls, letters, ledgers, and subscription lists, there has emerged an important literature that illuminates the past of the first Jewish congregation and the beginning of Jewish life in America.

Congregation Shearith Israel, also known as the Spanish-Portuguese Synagogue, has maintained its distinctly Sephardic identity. The synagogue appears here in beauty and solemnity, decorated with flowers and ferns for the festival of Yom ha-Bikkurim, the Day of the First Fruits.

The small chapel, embellished with heirlooms from the first synagogue, is a cherished shrine of colonial Jewry. The Tablets of the Ten Commandments and the two vases over the Ark, the perpetually burning lamp hanging before it, the large candlesticks and some of the benches came from the Mill Street Synagogue and are still used here. In the Ark repose Sacred Scrolls which suffered damage in the Revolutionary War but were later restored.

Shearith Israel is still vigorous in spirit after three hundred years of existence, and continues to be an eminent center of community life, attractive to its own congregants and to a host of outside admirers as well. Its modern community house provides facilities to young and old for religious training and social fellowship. The congregational auxiliaries engage in a wide range of activities directed toward nurturing the Jewish way of life. Its Hebrew Relief Society, the several clubs for men, women, young married couples, college students, and young girls, and its various committees, are all dedicated to furthering the extensive congregational program. When the Shearith Israel League presents one of its many offerings, for example, the yearly music festival performed by the congregation's choral group, an overflow audience is present to enjoy the musical event. The chorus is particularly devoted to the perpetuation of Sephardic liturgical melodies and traditional songs.

Many generations have passed through the religious school since it was established with the founding of Shearith Israel. It has become a distinguished Talmud Torah School, and many descendants of earlier congregants receive their religious training here, just as their forebears did, in close adherence to the Orthodox tradition. Its classes now embrace the tenth generation, from the first-grader to teen-age boys and girls. When the students graduate from the school, a diploma and a Bible are bestowed upon them as an award from Shearith Israel's Talmud Torah School.

On Memorial Day of every year
the congregation and its friends
reverently remember those who rest
in eternal peace in the historic cemetery of Shearith Israel. Bordered by
old buildings on Chatham Square in
lower Manhattan, the site is famous
as the first Jewish cemetery in New
York and the second oldest in the
United States. The hallowed burial
ground was used by Congregation
Shearith Israel from 1682 to 1831 and
to this day it is a landmark of Old
New York. The ancient gravestones
disclose the renowned names of Jewish pioneers and patriotic supporters
of the American Revolution.

We have to pay a visit to Newport, Rhode Island to see the oldest Jewish cemetery in America. In the colony where the trailblazers of religious liberty gave a friendly reception to the Jewish settlers, they could lay their dead to rest in the burial ground that has been theirs since 1677. Located only a short walk from the historic Touro Synagogue of Congregation Jeshuat Israel, this is the graveyard that inspired the illustrious poet Longfellow to write his reflective stanzas on "The Jewish Cemetery at Newport." Noted personalities and their families from the early days of Rhode Island lie buried here; later the great philanthropist of national fame, Judah Touro, joined them in eternal sleep.

The second oldest congregation in America had its beginnings in the days when sturdy Jewish pioneers settled in Newport, Rhode Island. About fifteen Jewish families of Spanish-Portuguese background established Congregation Jeshuat Israel in 1658. Before that they had faced the horrors of the Inquisition. Having placed their trust in the New World, they named their religious community "Salvation of Israel." Enjoying the blessings of religious freedom, the Jewish settlers cultivated friendly relations with all the other colonists; they met for common worship in private homes and lived the righteous life they had yearned for. The small congregation was gradually reinforced by other Sephardic Jews from Spain, Portugal, Holland, and the West Indies, including some Marranos, forcibly converted Jews who secretly retained their Judaic faith as the flames of the Inquisition burned around them.

Eventually, the day arrived that has been a momentous one in the history of all early Jewish congregations. For the Hanukah festival in 1763 lights blazed in the newly erected synagogue of Jeshuat Israel. With the participation of guests representing all segments of the population, a splendid consecration ceremony took place in the structure which is today a National Shrine dedicated to holiness and to the spirit of American democracy.

The Touro Synagogue, landmark of colonial America, was named after its rabbi, Isaac Touro. It is the oldest Jewish house of worship and one of the most remarkable religious edifices in the United States. A Georgian-style building made of imported English brick and New England wood, it was erected on barren land on the outskirts of a small town; today it stands, intact and unchanged, in the center of a thriving city. The synagogue is situated at an angle to Touro Street, because the Ark was placed in the traditional manner, on the east wall of the square structure, toward Jerusalem. Soon it became a place closely identified with American history. In the years 1781 to 1784 the Rhode Island General Assembly met in this synagogue, and during George Washington's visit to Newport in 1781 a town meeting was held there. During that period also it served for the sessions of the State Supreme Court, and in 1790, George Washington was once more greeted by the congregation, this time as President of the United States.

The interior of the synagogue is a rare example of that supreme beauty which is created by utter simplicity. Without the shining richness of gold and marble, its many graceful details blend harmoniously. Plain white walls and hand-wrought brass candelabra, a domed ceiling painted light blue and dotted with silver stars, and the traditional interior arrangement done after the Sephardic synagogues in Amsterdam and London, fill with awe those who enter this colonial shrine.

The reading desk, raised above the floor in the center of the synagogue, is flanked by movable seats. When George Washington visited the place, he saw it as we see it today. The twelve Ionic columns, signifying the

twelve tribes of ancient Israel, lend great dignity to the hall. The slender
pillars, made of single tree trunks, rise to the ceiling of the synagogue and
support the women's gallery. The clock on the balcony came from London
and has been recording the time for almost two centuries.

The beautifully carved Holy Ark is crowned with the Tablets of the
Ten Commandments. Before it hang the Perpetual Light and two candelabra. Like all the others, these too are suspended from the ceiling, while
four brass candlesticks grace the rail before the Ark. The Torahs in the
Ark are of great antiquity; one of them is four centuries old and was brought
to Newport by the first Jewish arrivals, who carried it with them from
Spain through all their wanderings.

Members of the Youth Group of the Touro Synagogue, Newport, volunteer their services and offer information to thousands of visitors every year. Visited by people of all faiths from every part of America and from many foreign countries, this Jewish house of God leaves enduring impressions, reverent and historic, in the mind of everyone who sees it.

Two features stand out as symbols of epochal events, exemplifying two ages, one that was ended, the other that had begun. Underneath the reading desk is the entrance to a secret underground passage going toward the street, a reminder of the hunted existence of the Jews and the Marranos in Spain, who sought hidden shelters and secret tunnels to escape from the persecuting tribunals of the inquisitors.

Raising the eyes from this memento of the dreadful past, we see the enlarged reproduction hanging on the wall, a symbol of the opening up of new horizons. When the Father of our Country assumed the office of President, the good wishes of the Hebrew Congregation in Newport elicited his celebrated reply of August 21, 1790. In classic phrases he extolled the basic beliefs of American democracy and the guiding principle of religious freedom. He declared: "The citizens of the United States of America have

a right to applaud themselves for having given to mankind examples of an enlarged and liberal policy: a policy worthy of imitation. All possess alike liberty of conscience and immunities of citizenship. It is now no more that toleration is spoken of, as if it was by the indulgence of one class of people, that another enjoyed the exercise of their inherent natural rights. For happily the Government of the United States, which gives to bigotry no sanction, to persecution no assistance requires only that they who live under its protection should demean themselves as good citizens, in giving it on all occasions their effectual support."

Then George Washington went on to say: "May the children of the Stock of Abraham, who dwell in this land, continue to merit and enjoy the good will of the other Inhabitants;" and in words that recall the saying of the Prophet Micah, the President stated: "... while every one shall sit in safety under his own vine and figtree, and there shall be none to make him afraid." In the closing part of the letter we read the abiding hope President Washington expressed for all generations to come: "May the father of all mercies scatter light and not darkness in our paths, and make us all in our several vocations useful here, and in his own due time and way everlastingly happy."

The young guides are ever ready to answer the many questions put by the visitors to the Touro Synagogue. Its collection of religious objects from the colonial period include Torah tops and breastplates of various designs. These ornaments and other ritual objects of superb beauty are examples of the art of Jewish silversmiths who earned fame in eighteenth-century America, foremost among them being the renowned Myer Myers.

One of the Torah scrolls is an outstanding example of religious art. Its Hebrew characters are gracefully written by hand on tanned calfskin and illuminated with silver and washed gold. Noteworthy is a parchment scroll of the Book of Esther enclosed in a case of Palestinian olive wood. An interesting old painting is a copy of an original canvas preserved in London's Sephardic Synagogue; it shows the initial Hebrew words of the Ten Commandments with their Spanish translation between the lines, and Moses and Aaron flanking the twin tablets.

A unique object claims attention in the exhibition room of the Touro Synagogue: the ancient Matzoth board, the only one still preserved from olden days. This quaint instrument served the families in the preparation of the unleavened bread for the Passover. As a museum piece, it illustrates realistically the upsurge of the industrial age. On this board the housewives rolled out and flattened the dough into thin cakes which they then baked in their homes—a great contrast to the machines that make Matzoth today.

The air of antiquity and of religious dedication pervading the little synagogue in Newport makes the honor bestowed upon it by the United States Government even more fitting. In acknowledgment "of its national significance for the inspiration and benefit of the people of the United States," Touro Synagogue was designated in 1946 as a National Historic Site.

At the time that the infant Jewish communities were rising in New York and Newport, a trickling of Jewish settlers reached the other colonies. Some arrived in Pennsylvania even before William Penn established his sanctuary of brotherly love. Yet, as in other settlements, there, too, long years were to pass before the size of the Jewish community and its economic strength permitted the erection and maintenance of a synagogue building.

The Jews of Philadelphia founded their first congregation several decades before the Declaration of Independence. Congregation Mikveh Israel, "The Hope of Israel," was established in 1740, meeting at first for divine services in a small house. Efforts to build a synagogue came to fruition through a generous contribution from an eminent member, the patriot-banker Haym Salomon. Thus Pennsylvania's first and America's third synagogue was dedicated in 1782. At the present time Congregation Mikveh Israel is housed in a stately edifice enhanced by a classic façade with Greek columns and handsomely decorated porticos.

From the time of its founding Mikveh Israel has adhered to the Sephardic mode of worship. Its vast auditorium is suggestive of the Ortho-

dox synagogue with separate sections for men and women. But it may be noted that the women's gallery rises slightly from the main floor, creating a wide-open sweep around the broad Ark and its golden door.

The colonial simplicity of the interior conjures up historic memories. Rich in patriotic tradition, Mikveh Israel's past is linked with America's struggle for independence. Its congregants not only assisted in the peaceful development of Pennsylvania and crusaded for the founding of this nation, but served in large numbers as officers and in the ranks of the Revolutionary Army. With selfless generosity Haym Salomon made substantial monetary contributions toward carrying on the Revolution as he did for Mikveh Israel and the poor of Philadelphia. The strains of the war brought his religious home into financial distress, and he died in poverty himself. Fellow-citizens of all faiths came to the assistance of Mikveh Israel, and Benjamin Franklin was among the numerous celebrities whose names appear on the subscription list. This and other historic documents fill the archives of Mikveh Israel, including a letter from President Washington which, like the Newport letter, constitutes a revealing testimonial to Jewish history in America.

To the Hebrew Congregations in the Cities
of Philadelphia, New York, Charleston
and Richmond.

Gentlemen,

The liberality of sentiment towards
each other, which marks every political and religious denomination of men in this country,
stands unparalleled in the history of Nations. —
— The affection of such a people is a treasure beyond the reach of calculation; — and the re-
peated proofs which my fellow citizens have
given of their attachment to me, and approbation of my doings, form the purest source of
my temporal felicity. — The affectionate expressions of your address again excite my
gratitude, and receive my warmest acknowledgment. —
The Power and Goodness of the
Almighty were strongly manifested in the
events of our late glorious revolution; and
his

his kind interposition in our behalf has been no less visible in the establishment of our present equal Government:— In war he directed the Sword; and in peace he has ruled in our Councils.— My agency in both has been guided by the best intentions, and a sense of the duty which I owe my Country:— And as my exertions have hitherto been amply rewarded by the approbation of my fellow Citizens, I shall endeavour to deserve a continuance of it by my future conduct.

May the same temporal and eternal blessings which you implore for me, rest upon your Congregations.—

G: Washington

When George Washington was elected to be the first President of the United States, the Jewish congregations of Philadelphia, New York, Charleston, and Richmond jointly addressed him in a letter of felicitations. President Washington's reply reflects the sentiment he entertained for his supporters.

One of the several congregations that tendered congratulations to George Washington on his election to the Presidency was Kahal Kadosh Beth Elohim, "The Holy Congregation House of God," in Charleston, South Carolina. It prides itself on being the fourth oldest congregation in the United States. A landmark of picturesque Charleston, this Jewish house of worship represents the finest example of Greek revival architecture in the country. The structure, of subtle strength and beauty, enclosed by a wrought iron fence of delicate design, gleams brightly in the southern sun and proclaims over its doors in Hebrew and in English the Jewish credo of the universal God: "Hear O Israel, the Lord our God is the sole Eternal Being."

Jews were among the first colonists who went to South Carolina soon after its founding. In the second quarter of the eighteenth century they settled in larger numbers there, and in 1750 Beth Elohim was established in Charleston. Illustrious citizens were members of the congregation, which followed the Orthodox Sephardic tradition. The names of Jews in

colonial Charleston appear on the pages of history. Two of the most distinguished came from London: Moses Lindo, pioneer and developer of the colony's great indigo industry, and young Francis Salvador, hero of the Revolution and the first Jew to give his life for this country's independence.

Later, greatly augmented in membership by immigrants from Germany, Beth Elohim had a large and prosperous congregation. It was the first American congregation to adopt reform in worship and to change the structural form of the synagogue's interior. When the old synagogue burned down and the present one was built in 1840, the customary disposition, in which the reading desk was placed off the Ark on the floor, gave way to a then novel construction. A move to install an organ and to seat men and women together won favor with the congregants. Beth Elohim in Charleston then introduced other innovations; its actions became known as the Reform Movement, later adopted by several Jewish congregations in America.

Richmond's is the fourth of the Hebrew Congregations to which
President Washington referred in his letter of acknowledgment. This gives
evidence of a long, unbroken history of Jewish life in Richmond, Virginia
because it shows that Congregation Beth Shalome, "House of Peace," ex-
isted there in those years. Individual Jewish settlers are known to have
lived in Virginia more than a century before the Revolution, but a great
fire destroyed the early minute books of Beth Shalome, and the congregation's origin was lost to history. At the present time Congregation Beth
Ahabah, "the House of Love," continues as the heir of Beth Shalome in
Richmond, Virginia. Founded in 1841, it was greatly enlarged when the
membership of old Beth Shalome joined it in a body in 1898, bringing
their Torahs and synagogue equipment. The united congregations' new
house of prayer, which it still occupies today, was dedicated in 1904.

In Georgia, the last of the thirteen colonies, Jews settled in Savannah in 1733, the same year that General Oglethorpe laid out that town. They were highly praised by the Governor as outstanding contributors to the colony's economy. The Torah they brought with them is still in the possession of Congregation Mickve Israel in Savannah, Georgia. At first worship was conducted in private rooms. The colonial community was temporarily dissolved, then revived in 1774, and received a perpetual charter in 1790. From that year to this, Mickve Israel's history has been faithfully recorded, relating the erection of the first synagogue building in Georgia in 1820 and the construction of two later ones, including the present Gothic structure which has housed the historic congregation since 1878.

Jews trekked along with other pioneers and helped to push back the frontiers of the United States, pouring their religious faith and creative energy into the building of America. Judah Touro was one of the first settlers who went from the East to New Orleans in 1802. The son of the rabbi of the Newport Synagogue, he was successful in business, using his wealth to aid numerous public institutions throughout the land and to assist the growing community of American Jews.

In 1828 Jewish settlers of German origin in New Orleans founded Congregation Gates of Mercy, the forerunner of the present congregation, and twelve years later the Spanish-Portuguese community organized Congregation Dispersed of Judah. Touro extended his kindness to both, and when they merged in 1881, the brotherly union assumed the name "Touro Synagogue of New Orleans," in tribute to the memory of their common patron. It is the oldest Jewish congregation in the Mississippi Valley. The present dome-capped house of worship is a beautiful memorial to the great patriot and philanthropist who was severely wounded in the War of 1812. Nursed back to health, he lived long and worked hard, devoting his whole fortune to the good causes he was eager to support, including the Bunker Hill Monument, public libraries, churches, parks, hospitals, universities, and orphan asylums, not forgetting the Newport Synagogue and the cemetery, where, in accordance with his wish, his remains are at rest beside his mother's.

CHAPTER THREE

THE
JEWISH HOUSE
OF WORSHIP

"This is none other than the house of
God, and this is the gate of heaven."
(*Genesis* 28:17)

Jews in America have participated wholeheartedly in the formation of American civilization from the beginning of its history. Most of the early Jewish colonists were of Spanish and Portuguese origin; Jewish emigrants from West European and later from Central and East European countries subsequently joined them in building the Jewish community. About four thousand congregations are scattered over the country, and the houses the Jews have built to God are as diverse in external appearance as are the backgrounds of the congregations. Wherever they have come from, Jews believe in the same Mosaic ideals and religious aspirations, but their synagogues, as religious expressions in architectural form, are widely divergent.

Some of the newcomers carried with them memories of synagogues they had known in the Old World. During their long march through history the Jews have been inclined to adopt for synagogue structures the architectural patterns of their environment, and like other religious groups, they transplanted these old historical styles to newborn America. Various patterns have left their imprint on American synagogues. Thus, for instance, in Isaiah Temple of Chicago, Illinois, the dome, the slender tower, the decorative pattern of the walls bring to mind Mediterranean art. The Tablets of the Law cut above the doors is the symbol which identifies the building as a Jewish house of worship.

The architecture of the many synagogues from Maine to California manifests no specifically Jewish style. The synagogue of B'nai Jacob, "The Sons of Jacob," in New Haven, Connecticut, reveals strong Byzantine features, twin towers and oriental ornamentations. Crowned by two Stars of David, the edifice represents a style that gained popularity throughout the second half of the last century and still reappears in new variations.

Elaborate and ornate is Boston's Ohabei Shalom, "The Lovers of Peace" (top), an imposing structure designed for a large congregational family. Its domed auditorium and high façade are in sharp contrast to the architectural pattern chosen by another large community, Congregation Mt. Sinai Anshe Emeth, "The Mt. Sinai People of Truth," in New York City (bottom.)

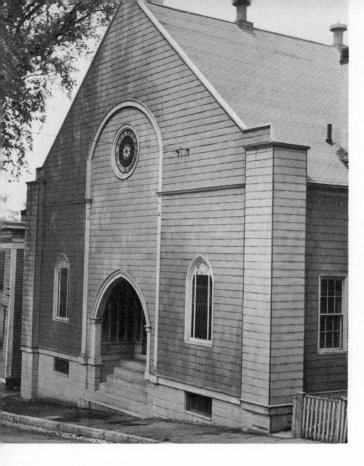

In the towns and in rural areas small synagogues grew out of the local scene. A Jewish house of prayer can function only where there are a sufficient number of Jewish families to provide the quorum of at least ten men required to be present for public worship. Colonial simplicity marks Synagogue Beth Jacob, "The House of Jacob," in Plymouth, Massachusetts (top), and a humble wood structure houses Synagogue Adath Israel, "Children of Israel," in Newton, Connecticut (bottom).

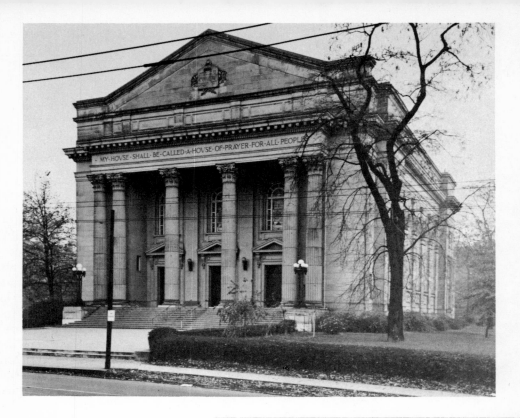

The architectural form of the classic school is reflected in the synagogue of Congregation Bene Israel, "The House of Israel," in Cincinnati, Ohio (top). Lofty Greek columns dominate its massive body, quite unlike the spacious edifice that serves the East Midwood Jewish Center in Brooklyn, New York (bottom). The swelling number of such centers, ministering to the religious and social needs of the Jewish community, indicate the role synagogues assume in the American environment.

The very harmonious blending of a dome bounded with plain, straight lines places emphasis on the old and the new. Temple Emanu-El, "God Is With Us," in Providence, Rhode Island (top), exemplifies a trend toward restrained innovations in synagogue structures. These novel forms conform with the contemporary approach in general architecture in America. The sober walls display Jewish emblems. In keeping with the trend, similar smooth lines prevail in the house of worship of Congregation Ohav Sholaum, "The Lovers of Peace," in New York City (bottom).

The architectural form of certain new synagogues reveals a fusion of tradition with modernity. Religious elements and utilitarian considerations have created structures with impressive halls of worship and adjoining centers for educational and social activities. Thus Congregation B'nai Israel, "The Sons of Israel," in Millburn, New Jersey (top), built its synagogue with blank walls and walls embellished with religious symbols. Most prominent of the representations is the Burning Bush which Moses saw before he received the Decalogue. Another congregation, Beth Israel, "The House of Israel," in Lebanon, Pennsylvania, followed the example of modernity, adopting a design defined by clear lines and untrammelled contours (bottom).

Prompted by devotion to God, religious fervor has planted synagogues in the less attractive areas of congested sections of large cities. Frequently small groups, with a common background, bound by ties of national or local origin, come together in rented rooms to continue their own congregations. Such a one is Congregation Tel Aviv, "The Hill of Spring," which flourishes in an old-fashioned brownstone house in downtown New York.

Determined to fulfill their religious duties on weekdays when engaged in business, members of some occupational groups worship in synagogues they maintain near their shops and stores. In the very heart of New York's bustling trade centers, the furriers, the millinery and the garment workers have established synagogues, and so also have actors and stagehands in Broadway's theatrical district.

59

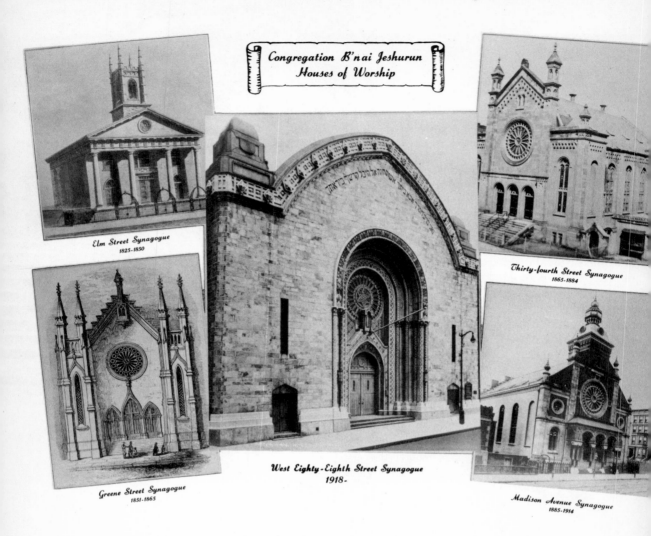

Congregation B'nai Jeshurun
Houses of Worship

Elm Street Synagogue
1825-1850

Greene Street Synagogue
1851-1865

West Eighty-Eighth Street Synagogue
1918-

Thirty-fourth Street Synagogue
1865-1884

Madison Avenue Synagogue
1885-1914

Many congregations can look back on a long past, but there are only two in America that have retained their original structures on their original sites—only those in Newport and Charleston have withstood changing conditions. As a result of the dynamic life and progress in the United States, challenged by industrial and commercial expansion in towns and cities, most congregations have followed the shifting population, leaving old sections and erecting new synagogues in more appropriate locations. A noteworthy example of this general process of change conditioned by urban development is Congregation B'nai Jeshurun, "The Sons of Righteousness," New York's second oldest Jewish congregation. More than a hundred years old, B'nai Jeshurun now carries out its high purpose in the fifth of its synagogue buildings.

With increased immigration, the congregations often outgrew the synagogue's capacity, and larger houses of worship had to be erected to satisfy the needs of the expanding community. Four structures served the century-old Congregation Emanu-El in New York prior to its occupancy of the present edifice. As in other congregations, pictures of earlier buildings can be seen on the walls of its Community House, testifying to steady change, growth, and efficient ministry. Pride in the past has led to the assembling of interesting memorabilia in congregational collections. The memory of the founders, of former spiritual leaders and benevolent laymen, lives on in picture galleries, and ceremonial objects used by past generations are treasured and displayed in exhibits.

The exterior of the synagogue has never followed any rigid form, but its interior arrangement is more strictly governed by an established plan. Timeless and unchanging features greet the eyes when viewing the interior of the synagogue. Congregation Shaaray Tefila, "The Gates of Prayer," in Far Rockaway, New York, dedicated in 1953, retains the traditional pattern of earlier ages. The Bimah, an elevated platform for the reading of the Torah, is separated from the Ark, the floor stands open, and the seats fan out on both sides.

Numerous references in the Bible relate to the building of the Tabernacle, the tent in which the Ark of the Covenant was deposited during the wandering in the wilderness. The Scriptures also mention some features of the Temple in Jerusalem. A modern replica of the Ark, the Aron Hakodesh stands as an indispensable element in every Jewish house of worship and is always the most important part of the synagogue. As in Biblical times, suspended in front of the Ark burns the flame of the Ner Tamid, symbol of the Eternal Light which is retained in and emanates from the Torah. Placed over the Ark, the Tablets of the Law are seen in every synagogue, symbolizing the Revelation on Mount Sinai and Judaism's message to the world. A Hebrew inscription on the Ark reminds us of the holiness of the sanctuary. Most frequently it reads: "Know before Whom thou standest."

The need for a large seating capacity in the face of adverse building conditions imposed by big cities forced deviations from the traditional plan of the synagogue. Most of the present-day structures combine the Ark with the reading desk while the floor is given over completely to seats facing the Ark.

With some exceptions, in Sephardic synagogues, seven-branched Menorahs flank the Ark. The candelabrum, universal symbol of the spiritual light which God has bestowed on Israel, was a fixture of the Tabernacle and of the Temple, also. Its counterpart is displayed in most synagogues, and so is the Mogen Dovid, the six-pointed star known as the Shield of David. Though not mentioned in the Bible, it stands as the emblem of the whole Jewish people. The most sacred symbol of Judaism, the Sefer Torah, the Scroll of the Law, is housed in the Ark, occupying the dominant place in the synagogue. Because of its supreme sanctity the Sefer Torah is reverently treasured in beautiful sanctuaries. For example, in the Synagogue B'nai Jeshurun (below) the Ark is enriched with the rare beauty of ancient Semitic art, composed of arresting designs derived from the remnants of buildings in Palestine and Moorish Spain.

Symbolic representations in some modern synagogues illustrate certain basic beliefs of Judaism. Living up to the Second Commandment, "Thou shalt not make unto thee a graven image," synagogues exclude every figure suggestive of idolatry, restricting their symbolism to divine truth and religious hope. In the Stephen Wise Free Synagogue in New York, for example, basic teachings of Judaism are translated into striking designs. The Sabbath and the holy days are given visible expression on the arch that embraces the Ark, and panels on both sides explain Jewish tenets and ideals.

One of the panels reminds us of the fact that the Torah reveals the eternal Truth. It is the Word of God that nurtured and maintained the Jewish people throughout the ages. Hence the ornament of the open Scroll bearing the word Emet or Truth significantly carries the grateful words recited in the prayer: "Praised be He Who has given the Law to His people Israel, in holiness."

"Praised be Thou, O Lord, Who blessest His people Israel with peace." Peace is the very spirit of the Jewish faith. In a symbolic way the Biblical dove and olive branch reappear with the Hebrew letter Shin, signifying Shalom as well as Shaddai, the common word for peace and for God's name.

The ideals permeating Jewish life and motivating Jewish strivings are fervently pronounced in the prayer: "Praised be Thou, O Lord the King, Who loveth righteousness and justice." The traditional symbol of the scales gains added meaning through the letter Mem in the center of the representation, standing for Mishpat, the Hebrew sign of Justice.

The quotation from the Ethics of the Fathers, "On Torah, on labor, and on deeds of loving kindness," sums up the Jewish way of life. This composition combines the scroll, the pitchfork and sickle, the wheat and the bread, and a split coin as well. It suggests Tzedakah or Charity, the Jew's obligation to justice which he must practice by donating part of his possessions for the welfare of the whole community.

Study and learning have kept alive the Torah, and in return, the Torah has imparted religious faith and spiritual vigor to those who have sought its knowledge. The Law and the Decalogue have inspired superb achievements throughout history, proving the truth that "The study of the Law is equal to all else."

The ideals of human dignity and liberty expounded in the Hebrew Scriptures have inspired our great democracy and blessed our land. The message engraved on the Liberty Bell was taken from the *Book of Leviticus* 25:10: "Proclaim liberty throughout the land unto all the inhabitants thereof," words that were symbolized by the sound of the bell when it rang out in America. The Hebraic tradition of democracy and the devotion of Jews to its principles are symbolically presented in the Stephen Wise Free Synagogue.

Whether modest or magnificent, all Jewish houses of worship have come into existence through the desire and effort of individuals whose yearning for a religious home brought about the founding of a synagogue. Small and large, Orthodox, Conservative and Reform, the elevating spirit and warmth of Jewish worship dwell even in the simplest prayer room: some contain no more than the Ark of the Torah and a few chairs.

Loyalty to their faith and reverence toward God are maintained by the Jewish members of the Armed Forces in the most distant lands. Religious services on Army posts and far battlefields impart spiritual strength and the feeling of home to the men. Holiday services are held in military installations across the States and over the world, in camp chapels and makeshift sanctuaries. Some of those in the hills of Korea look like open-air synagogues, where Hebrew prayers and chants soar into the vastness of space as Jewish soldiers congregate to celebrate the holidays.

Both ignorance and cruelty burned the synagogues in the lands of torture and persecution. After the heroic landing in Normandy, Jewish servicemen paused in an apple orchard to give thanks and to implore the Almighty for the return of justice and mercy. Tyranny had to capitulate to liberty, and religious freedom in liberated Europe signaled the rebirth of the synagogue. Among our troops in Austria, Jewish soldiers, who helped to fight for democracy, participated with gladdened hearts in the historic Jewish New Year celebration held in Salzburg, the first in the wake of victory.

CHAPTER FOUR

THE

CELEBRATION

OF THE SABBATH

"Observe the Sabbath day, to keep it holy,
as the Lord thy God commanded thee."
(*Deuteronomy* 5:12)

The genius of the Mosaic faith established the Temple in Jerusalem and many smaller synagogues throughout the Holy Land, where the people regularly assembled to worship God. Judaism instituted profound prayers which expressed the beliefs, the ideals, and the hopes Jews harbored in their souls and uttered in His house, as they still do today. For the worship of God, one day in every week was set apart as the Sabbath and many more days during the year as holidays. These observances have been maintained by Jews all over the world from antiquity up to the present.

Ranking high in significance is the Sabbath, enjoined on the Jew as strongly as it is proclaimed by the incisive phrases in the Ten Commandments: "Remember the sabbath day, to keep it holy. Six days shalt thou labor, and do all thy work; but the seventh day is a sabbath unto the Lord thy God, in it thou shalt not do any manner of work, thou, nor thy son, nor thy daughter, nor thy man-servant, nor thy maid-servant, nor thy cattle, nor thy stranger that is within thy gates; for in six days the Lord made heaven and earth, the sea, and all that in them is, and rested on the seventh day; wherefore the Lord blessed the sabbath day, and hallowed it."

The Jewish religion calls on every Jew to meet God in common and public worship at the synagogue. To maintain order in the liturgy each congregation uses a prayer book of its own choosing. Many Jewish prayers go back two thousand years and more, and there have been prayer books, too, of ancient times. The traditional prayer book in use today traces its ancestry back to the ninth century. Owing to the fact that American Jews originate from many countries, the congregations differ to some degree in their prayer books and synagogical practices.

We may observe deviations in the customs of Orthodox, Conservative, and Reform congregations. Many synagogues recite all the prayers in Hebrew, some pray partly in English, but in all synagogues the most sacred portions of the liturgy are always intoned in Hebrew. Every Orthodox and Conservative congregation insists that the head be covered during religious services, while the Reform branch, with some exceptions, departs from this tradition. In Orthodox synagogues men and women sit apart, and organ music is strictly frowned upon. In other synagogues an organ and a choir participate in divine services.

Whatever the shade of Jewish expression, the celebration of the Sabbath stands out as an exalted source of inspiration shared through immortal prayers and beautiful hymns. We shall witness ceremonial highlights common to the liturgy of all Orthodox, Conservative, and Reform congregations. Here we follow the Sabbath worship and the prayers paraphrased from the Hebrew. This condensed form reflects the essence of the ritual rather than the specific liturgy of a particular group of congregations. The sanctification of the Sabbath, the reading of the Torah, the rabbi's sermon, the adoration, and the benediction unfold the reverent mood, the religious thoughts, and the sublime spirit which distinguish Jewish worship in every synagogue.

The Sabbath, ushered in on Friday evening, is welcomed with the Psalm: "O come, let us sing unto the Lord, let us joyfully acclaim the Rock of our salvation. Let us approach Him with thanksgiving, and acclaim Him with songs of praise...." The worship takes its course with prayers intoned by the rabbi, chants sung by the cantor, the congregation's responses in unison, and the singing of hymns.

When the service advances to the appropriate place, the cantor lifts a cup of wine and consecrates the Sabbath: "Let us praise God with this symbol of joy, and thank Him for the blessings of the past week, for life and strength, for home and love and friendship, for the discipline of our trials and temptations, for the happiness that has come to us out of our labors. Thou hast ennobled us, O God, by the blessings of work, and in love hast sanctified us by the Sabbath rest and worship as ordained in the Torah...."

With this ceremony at the synagogue and also in Jewish homes, the Sabbath is formally inaugurated.

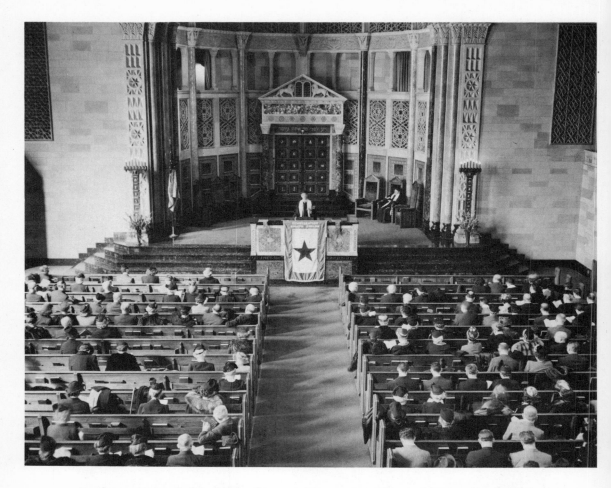

At the outset of the Sabbath morning service the reader gives thanks to God for the gift of the Sabbath day and calls the congregation to worship. Following the recital of the opening prayers and passages from Psalms, the worshippers turn to God, who is King, Redeemer, and Helper, confessing that no human tongue alone can exhaust His praises, and, therefore, all the people shall unite in extolling His name. The summons goes out for common worship by all the congregants, in order to pay homage to God, the Creator of the whole universe, Who has given the Torah to the people of Israel and entrusted them with the Divine Message. In the first part of the service many of the same prayers are uttered that Jews also say on every weekday. These prayers testify to their faith in God, and petition Him that He grant peace, well-being, and blessing to the world. Having implored His mercy, loving kindness, forgiveness, and protection, the worshippers plead for God's acceptance of the prayers that they offer Him.

Two supreme prayers penetrate the conscience of the Jewish people. Since antiquity Jews have pronounced their phrases from childhood to the end of life. Both are recited in various parts of the daily worship and in the Sabbath service as well: "The Shema," Israel's Confession of Faith, and "The Kaddish," the prayer for the glorification of the Almighty and for the coming of the Kingdom of God. Immediately after the beginning of the Sabbath service the reader intones the Shema and the Kaddish, and as the liturgy progresses, the congregation rises and joins in the prayer of sanctification: "Holy, holy, holy is the Lord of hosts, the earth is full of His glory. In all places of Thy dominion, Thy name is praised and glorified. The Lord shall reign forever. Thy God, O Zion, shall be Sovereign unto all generations. Hallelujah!"

Having concluded the prayers of supplication for peace, contentment, and love, the rabbi calls on the congregants for meditation and the reading of the silent prayer which begins: "O Lord, guard my tongue from evil, and my lips from speaking guile. . . ." Now the service arrives at the part that marks the central act of public worship, the reading of the Torah. The congregation stands reverently as the Torah is taken from the Ark and the basic creed of Judaism rings out with the vibrant chanting of the cantor: "Hear, O Israel, the Lord our God, the Lord is One." Then he continues: "And thou shalt love the Lord thy God with all thy heart, and with all thy soul, and with all thy might. . . ."

The Torah is divested of its ornaments and cover, and the Sacred Scroll unrolled on the reading desk. Traditionally, at the Sabbath morning service seven worshippers are given the honor of being called when the weekly portion from the Five Books of Moses is read to the assembly. In view of the Torah each of the honored men respectfully bows and pronounces the blessing: "Bless ye the Lord who is to be praised. Blessed is the Lord who is to be blessed for ever and ever." The congregation then responds by repeating the blessing, and the congregant at the reading desk continues: "Praised be Thou, O Lord our God, King of the universe Who has called us from all the peoples, and given us Thy Torah. Blessed are Thou, O Lord, Giver of the Torah."

The reading aloud from the Book of the Law in all public services has been a permanent institution since early Jewish history. In deference to the Word of God no common worship at the synagogue is conducted without the reading of the Hebrew Bible by one of the worshippers or the officiating reader.

In addition to the Torah reading, selections from the Haftorah, the Book of Prophets, are read. Upon the completion of the Torah reading and before going on to the Haftorah, the congregation rises. As a symbolic act of submission and reaffirmation, the Torah is lifted up and the pronouncement made: "And this is the Law which Moses set before the children of Israel by the command of the Lord!"

Near the end of the Torah service the rabbi offers his prayer for the congregation and the country. He implores a blessing on all the members and their families, that they may be helped in their needs and difficulties. He prays for the reward of joy for those who are charitable and merciful, who aid the poor, care for the sick, teach the people, and extend a helping hand to those who have lost their way in the world. The rabbi invokes a blessing upon the nation and petitions God to enlighten with wisdom and to bless with courage, vision, and high purpose those whom the people have set in authority, the President, his counselors, the judges, the law-givers, and the executives, that they may rule wisely and justly. In closing he utters a supplication for peace and good-will among all the inhabitants of the country and for the spread of religion, that the nation may be exalted in righteousness, with world-peace and justice for all.

Two worshippers are called to the reading desk to replace the cover and ornaments on the Sacred Scroll before it is returned to the Ark. When the reader takes up the Torah, the people rise, and as the Scroll is returned to the Ark, they chant together: " . . . His majesty is above the earth and heaven, He hath given glory unto His people, praise to all His faithful ones, to the children of Israel, a people near to Him. Hallelujah!"

As in many cases, in his sermon the rabbi refers to Biblical stories and to current events, elaborating on the Jew's duty to view the problems of daily life in the light of the Mosaic precepts and to approach their solution in the spirit of justice and good-will. At the end of the sermon the Ark is opened for the act of adoration. The assembly stands and recites the prayer that proclaims God as the Supreme King of the universe and as God of a united humanity: "...He is our God, there is none else.... We bow the head and bend the knee and magnify the King of kings, the Holy One, blessed be He...."

Near the conclusion of the worship the moving rite takes place that occurs at the end of every service and binds the generations in piety toward their departed. The rabbi introduces the Kaddish by recalling those loved ones who have departed from sight but who are not dead so long as the thought of them inspires the living; they still live on earth in the acts of goodness they performed and in the hearts of those who cherish their memory. The rabbi asks the mourners to rise and in submission to God's will to recite the Kaddish: "Magnified and sanctified be His great name throughout the world which He hath created according to His will.

May He establish His kingdom in your life-time and in your days, and during the life-time of all the house of Israel, speedily and at a near time; and say ye, Amen." While the mourners continue with the Kaddish, the thoughts of everyone present go out to those who repose in eternity.

The congregation now rises to sing the "En Kelohenu," the great anthem of sweeping cadences: "There is none like our God, there is none like our Lord, there is none like our King, there is none like our Savior. . . ." When the last strains die away, the rabbi raises his arms for the age-old rite of the benediction.

Facing the congregation, the rabbi pronounces the blessing which comes from the Hebrew Bible, *Numbers* 6:22-27, and which was also besought by the priests of ancient Israel: "And the Lord spoke unto Moses, saying: Speak unto Aaron and unto his sons, saying: On this wise ye shall bless the children of Israel; ye shall say unto them: The Lord bless thee, and keep thee; The Lord make His face to shine upon thee, and be gracious unto thee; The Lord lift up His countenance upon thee, and give thee peace. So shall they put My name upon the children of Israel, and I will bless them."

With this solemn benediction, the Sabbath morning service comes to a close.

While the morning service for adults is in progress in the main prayer hall, the Junior Congregation celebrates the Sabbath in the chapel. Through their studies in the Religious School, the young people have become familiar with the meaning of the Sabbath and its observance in the synagogue and at home. Prepared to participate in their own services, here they recite prayers, sing hymns, make responses, and preach short sermons. The older boys function as readers and lead the assembly through the Sabbath ritual.

The Junior Congregation stands on its own, conducting its services and assuming responsibilities in the Sanctuary. Like the adults, they read the Torah, the weekly lesson from it and from the Haftorah. The reader follows the text of the Torah with the pointer, which ends in a small hand and pointing finger. Proceeding from word to word and line to line, he reads the Hebrew text, following it with the English translation.

The Junior Congregation performs the traditional ritual of the Sabbath hallowed by the ages and geared to the proper comprehension of young boys and girls. Reaching deep into the soul, their Sabbath service gives flight to the spirit and the religious ideas of Judaism. Drawing on these, the children meditate upon God, perform religious acts and express faith and devotion through prayers and sermons they frequently compose themselves.

Jewish worship is permeated with the chanting of prayers and with the singing of hymns by the whole congregation. The quiet rhythm of the tender cantillations modulates into lofty tunes charged with deep emotion, and in a multitude of voices they express exalted sentiments. As a regular part of the synagogue service, the boys and girls join in the singing of loved phrases and sacred melodies, the customary Hebrew hymns, such as "Come O Sabbath," "Praise the Lord," "God is in His Holy Temple," "Hymn of Peace," "Our Father Our King," "O Jerusalem," the "Hatikvah" (Hope), and then the "Star Spangled Banner," "America," and "America the Beautiful." The Junior Congregation intones with vigor one of the most popular and universally sung hymns, the "Adon Olom." Cherished

by countless generations, the sublime thoughts and simple words of the "Lord of the World" echo down from time immemorial:

"Lord of the world, He reigned alone
While yet the universe was naught,
When by His will all things were wrought,
Then first His sovereign name was known.
And when the all shall cease to be
In dread lone splendor He shall reign,
He was, He is, He shall remain
In glorious eternity. . . ."

The prayers, the chants, and the Torah service, constituting a stately ceremony, convey to the young worshippers the beauty, the depth, and the decorum of the Sabbath service. Active throughout the whole ceremonial, now they move in a procession around the chapel to return the Torah to the Ark. The future generation is growing up with the knowledge that it is involved in great questions of life as individuals and as members of the community as well. The experience of the weekly Junior Service inspires the boys and girls to identify themselves with the message of the Sabbath: Man's homage to God, peace, justice, and righteousness.

The Sabbath and the manner of celebrating it are quite different from the crude customs that prevailed among the peoples of the period when the Mosaic Law was revealed to Israel. The Sabbath day was to belong to God, and ever since in all places where Jews have lived throughout the long centuries, the Sabbath has been celebrated in divine services and by a thorough change of routine in the everyday life.

All work and material pursuits cease in order that the day may be dedicated to rest and spiritual enrichment. The sanctified Sabbath brings lightness of heart created through physical relaxation, meditation, prayer, and study. The weekly festival enters the home, making it joyful and dignified with the lighting of candles, the recital of prayers, the offering of blessings over festive meals, and the wearing of the best garments the family can afford in order to distinguish the Sabbath from the rest of the week. Traditionally, its coming is greeted with the Kiddush at home, and when the first stars appear in the sky, the exit of the Sabbath is observed by the Havdalah, a picturesque ceremony performed with a braided candle's torchlike flame, fragrant spices, and savory wine.

The Torah offers two explanations for the institution of the Sabbath: one, the creation of the world in six days and the designation of the seventh as the day of rest; and the other, the life of slavery in Egypt, where Jews were deprived of man's elementary need to replenish his energies and to be able to rise spiritually. The Sabbath proclaims the principles of human dignity and equality, and fulfills man's natural right to a day of release and refreshment.

These ideas were basically new when compared with those that governed society in Biblical times. They introduced a new concept of man and of his place on earth which God assigned to him when He created the world. The Sabbath is one of the great institutions that the Hebrews have given to mankind. The principles and rules taken for granted today took humanity tens of centuries to attain as it climbed higher in the progress of history.

The observance of the weekly commemoration of creation and rest implies more than abstention from work. It makes man free to devote himself to intellectual improvement. Actually, the Sabbath is a day for praying together at the synagogue, for expanding knowledge through instruction, and for the enjoyment of fellowship with other people.

While prayer in solitude is permissible, Judaism encourages common worship on every occasion when ten men are present, and makes mandatory attendance at the synagogue on the Sabbath and on holidays. Traditionally, members of the Jewish faith pray three times a day, in the morning, in the afternoon, and in the evening. On the Sabbath, too, they meet three times for public worship, with additional dedication to study and social fellowship.

The old Jewish custom of listening to lectures on the Sabbath afternoon and participating in group discussions at the synagogue's meeting room persists in our time in the observance of the Oneg Shabbat. Some congregations arrange for the "Enjoyment of the Sabbath" on Friday evening after services, others on Saturday afternoon, when topics from Jewish lore and literature are on the program. Informal conversations, the serving of refreshments, and singing make the gathering joyful.

On the Sabbath afternoon the worshippers recite parts of the weekday prayers with additional prayers designed for the Sabbath, and read from the Sayings of the Fathers. The Torah is taken from the Ark, and three persons are called up for the reading of the first section of the weekly portion which will be read the following Sabbath morning. After the reading of the Torah mourners have the opportunity to perform the sacred act of reciting the Kaddish for their departed. Young and aged, rich and poor, mourners traditionally say the Kaddish at one of the synagogue services every day during the first eleven months after death, and then on every anniversary of the departure.

The Sabbath afternoon and evening services are comparatively short, yet integral parts of the majestic system of Jewish worship that celebrates the holy day. Prayers of praise, thanksgiving, affirmation, and petition rise up from earth to heaven and link daily human strivings with the Eternal and the Almighty. Thus we hear the worshippers pray on the Sabbath afternoon: "Our God and God of our fathers, accept our rest. Sanctify us by Thy commandment, and grant us our portion in Thy Torah. Satisfy us with Thy goodness, and gladden us with Thy salvation. Purify our hearts to serve Thee in truth. In Thy love and favor, O Lord our God, let us inherit Thy holy Sabbath, and may Israel who sanctify Thy name, rest thereon. Blessed art Thou, O Lord, who hallowest the Sabbath. . . ."

After sunset farewell is bidden to the Sabbath. The beautiful Havdalah ritual, performed at the synagogue and at home, ushers out the day of rest with benedictions over wine, sweet spices, and candlelight. Each of them a meaningful symbol of religious thoughts, their ceremonial use indicates the separation of the Holy from the Profane. The aroma of the spices is inhaled, the hands are spread toward the light which is then extinguished with wine, and leave is taken of the Sabbath with the chanting of the Havdalah blessings. This subtle ritual reminds us of the distinction between light and darkness, believers and heathen, the six days of the week and the seventh day, whose beneficence lingers on until the Sabbath is greeted again.

CHAPTER FIVE

THE

FAITH OF

THE FATHERS

"And Moses called unto all Israel, and said unto them:
Hear, O Israel, the statutes and the ordinances which
I speak in your ears this day, that ye may learn them,
and observe to do them." (*Deuteronomy* 5:1)

Judaism has always laid strong stress on the religious education of all the people and of each individual, and so the synagogue is concerned with the spiritual growth of young people from early childhood to the age when they have completed high school. The Religious School, an integral part of every congregation, inculcates in its pupils the faith of Israel and educates them in the customs and the traditions of the Jewish religion, its ideals, its history, and its literature. Through multifarious activities the school prepares children to share in the heritage that is theirs. In the environment of the synagogue active association with Jewish life and aspirations kindles a willingness in the young to fulfill the demands Judaism makes upon the Jew. The doors of the Religious School are open for instruction on weekday afternoons and on Sunday morning.

Courses in Jewish studies are closely integrated with the experience of fellowship with religionists. As the children grow older, increasing knowledge of the ancestral faith strengthens an awareness of themselves and of their responsibilities to the community. In the Religious School youngsters begin to devote themselves to worthy causes. They learn about God and His commandments, about the higher values of life taught in the Torah and expounded by the prophets and sages. There, too, friendships are developed, many of which will endure for years, some even extending over a lifetime.

Awakening to the wonders of the world and the adventures of life, small boys and girls become acquainted with some of the leading figures of Jewish history. Story-telling, songs, and dances playfully introduce the children to religious observances, and they celebrate the Sabbath and the festivals in their own jolly manner. Eagerly the little ones respond to prayers in Hebrew and English. Every Friday afternoon they set up their miniature synagogue, and while one of them officiates as rabbi, the rest join in prayers and singing. The children learn to observe the sanctity of the Sabbath, which imparts a festive spirit to the home where the family gathers for the Sabbath ritual. They will now proceed with the traditional blessing over a cup of wine, and they say grace over the Challahs, the loaves of twisted bread.

Top: "Sabbath, Sabbath, candles are lighted. Sabbath, Sabbath candles are lighted, the Sabbath is here."

Bottom: "Shalom, Shalom to you and to you! Shalom, Shalom, how do you do? How do you do?"

The creative urge and the manual skill of the youngsters both find expression in the making of ceremonial objects, which are used in the synagogue and in the home. Artcrafts correlated with classroom instruction afford opportunities for making a variety of objects. One of the most challenging is the little Torah with the handwritten and ornamented scroll, the ancient form of a book.

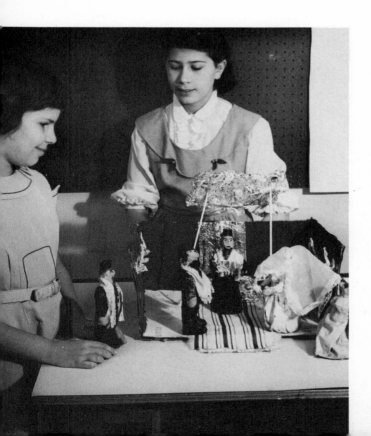

All children like to portray the heroes of the Bible and to recreate events from Jewish life. Deft in making figurines and in reconstructing religious scenes and rituals, through organized art projects they bring to life many themes. Stirred by the story of the arrival of the first Jews in New Amsterdam, some are engaged in reproducing their figures in clay statuettes, while others delight in making a Chupah and depicting the marriage ceremony with all the participants under the canopy.

Children draw colorful maps throughout the year. They depict Biblical narratives and particular features of the festivals as they come along on the Jewish calendar.

Dialogue and characters in puppet shows point up the meaning of religious tenets. Fun and learning are intermingled in the droll acting and speeches of the flouncing figures. Frequently performed in Hebrew, these absorbing puppet plays are helpful in learning the sacred tongue.

The youngsters keep busy, giving free flow to their imagination when they decorate the classrooms for festivals and parties. They eagerly make toys and games and design greeting cards appropriate to the holiday season to send to friends and relatives.

Abounding in great leaders and momentous events, Jewish history reaches back into the remote past for nearly four thousand years. The oldest of all recorded history is described in the Holy Scriptures of the Hebrews and its highlights are taught in every religious school. The children learn the past of a very ancient people, whose fate evolved between high glory and deep sorrow. It is a history steeped alternately in peace and in war, prosperity and want, unity and division, persecution and the struggle for liberty.

By tracing events and locating the sites of incidents on maps of the Holy Land, the periods of the patriarchs, the kings, and the prophets become real, and thus the sources of Judaism emerge in full perspective. Classroom journeys through the fascinating lands of the Middle East provide knowledge of the ancestors who brought forth the religious teachings that are immortalized in the Hebrew Bible and have lighted the path of a hundred generations.

With the destruction of the Second Temple in 70 C.E., the history of the Jews shifted from Palestine and continued in many countries where centers of Jewish learning were established. Prior to the dispersion and afterward, sages and rabbis, some earning their livelihood as wood-cutters, shepherds, and laborers, managed to maintain high religious and intellectual standards. Their lives make fascinating stories and their scholarship produced writings that are among the gems of the post-Biblical literature. Striking drawings made by the pupils picture the stories of Hillel, Johanan Ben Zakkai, Rabbi Akiba, and other sages who made great contributions to Jewish studies.

The history of the Jews then continues through the centuries: the Golden Age in Spain, the period of the Middle Ages in Europe, the Crusades, the Inquisition and the Emancipation, and later times of privation in ghettos and martyrdom suffered at the hands of dehumanized persecutors. The children's knowledge of American history is enhanced by learning the history of the Jews in this country. They are told about the role Jews played in the discovery and settlement of the New World, of the waves of immigration to the United States and the many contributions Jews made to our country's growth, as well as of their interest in the return of Jews to the Holy Land and the building of the State of Israel.

The historical significance and the spiritual meaning of the holidays and festivals are impressed upon young minds as these days draw near on the Jewish calendar. As symbols of beliefs and expressions of ethical ideals, they convey the teachings of Judaism. Impressive ceremonies enrich and inspire those who participate in them. Rosh Hashanah, the Jewish New Year, calls for a spiritual accounting, for self-examination and worthy resolutions. The Shofar is sounded to arouse the Jews to their duty to God and to man. On the holiest of all holidays, at the conclusion of Yom Kippur, the Day of Atonement or Day of Judgment, the ram's horn is blown again, marking the end of the High Holy Days with the recital of prayers for the happiness of all peoples and the well-being of all mankind.

Many pages of history are relived on Succoth, the Feast of Tabernacles. The young people of the Religious School lend a hand in the construction of the Succah, the booth reminiscent of the forty years of wandering in the wilderness and dwelling in rude huts. The Succah, covered with plants and shrubs and hung with fruits and vegetables, also commemorates the gathering of the harvest and is a thanksgiving festival. The Succah party at the school, when all the children gather at the Succah, is an unforgettable experience. The Lulab, a palm branch tied together with myrtle and willow branches, and the Etrog, a citron, both are symbolically carried while prayers and blessings are recited. The last day of Succoth is the occasion of a joyous pageantry: it is Simchath Torah, the Rejoicing of the Law, when the reading of the last weekly portion of the Torah is completed at the synagogue and the first chapters are started over again.

Preparing for the Passover season and observing the Seder ceremony are as old as the millennia that have passed since the Jews were liberated from their Egyptian bondage. The story of Passover, the Festival of Freedom, captivates the young with its sweeping narrative and the ancient mode of recalling a memorable event in Jewish history. From the Haggadah, the Passover Ritual Book, they learn the epic of the Exodus and the traditional celebration of the holiday at the Seder Table. Prayers of gratitude and songs of praise are uttered, and Matzoth, together with the other prescribed foods, is eaten in remembrance of the delivery from slavery. The Passover home ritual at the Seder supper and the reading of the Haggadah recall the birth of and reaffirm the dedication of the Jews to freedom.

The model Seder given at the Religious School brings to the pupils the practical experience and understanding of the ritual. At the dignified observance all the children actively partake in the symbolic acts performed with the unleavened bread, the parsley, the bitter herbs, the mixture of apples, nuts, spices and wine, the shank bone, the roasted egg, and the four cups of ceremonial wine.

During the festival of Hanukah, the Feast of Light or the Feast of Dedication, candles are lighted in every Jewish home on eight consecutive evenings. Historically, this holiday is associated with the rededication of the Temple in the year 168 B.C. following the reconquest of Jerusalem by the Maccabees. Because of their victory, the Temple could be cleansed of the pagan worship introduced into it by the Greco-Syrian rulers, and the Torah, the light of Israel, re-established in its place. The relighting of the Menorah in the Temple recalls this happy event. In keeping with it a happy atmosphere pervades the schools and homes, games are played, and gifts exchanged.

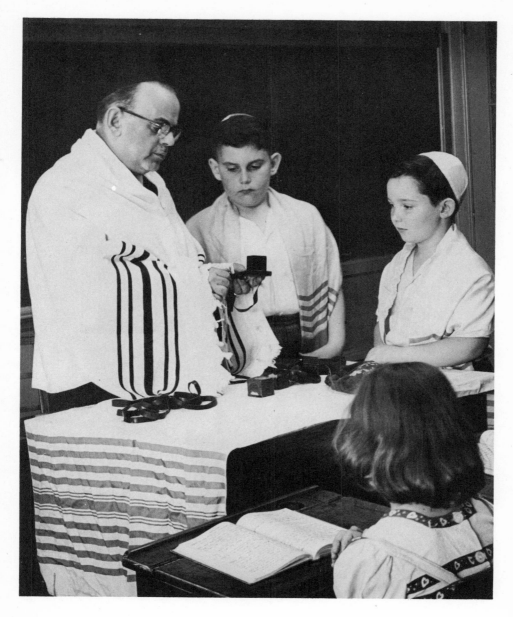

The prayer shawl and the phylacteries are introduced to boys who approach their thirteenth year. Both are to be donned in fulfillment of Biblical precepts to remind Jews of their religion. The Tallit, the prayer shawl with fringed ends, is worn for the morning prayer and at synagogue services as well. The Tefillin consists of two square boxes containing parchments inscribed with several verses from the books of Exodus and Deuteronomy commanding: "Thou shalt bind them for a sign upon thy hand, and they shall be for frontlets between thine eyes."

The same chapter of the Bible dealing with the Tefillin, Deuteronomy 6:9, also enjoins: "And thou shalt write them upon the door-posts of thy house, and upon thy gates." On the right of the entrance to a Jewish home is placed the Mezuzah, an enclosed parchment on which are written basic teachings of Judaism. The children have learned to recite them by heart: the Shema, the pronouncement on the omnipotence of God, and the duty of the Jew to teach the children His commandments.

Top: Inspired by the Torah and the liturgy, Jewish artisans have produced exquisite examples of ceremonial objects. Many of them are now collected and exhibited in institutions of Jewish learning. Arks, Torah scrolls, crowns and head pieces, mezuzahs, spice-boxes, kiddush cups, illuminated Haggadahs, and other relics many centuries old, originating in various countries where Jews have lived, are shown and explained to youngsters visiting the Jewish Museum in New York.

Right: Several attractive objects intrigue the young visitors, especially those which they try to make themselves in artcrafts. One of these is a Hanukah candlestick decorated with animal symbols. More than two hundred years old and once used in the Synagogue of Odessa in Russia, it is here an object of admiration.

Top: Future homemakers receive instruction in the dietary practices of the Jewish home. Cooking in conformity with Biblical dietary laws and preparing the customary food for the festivals constitute some of the workshop activities the girls pursue with pleasure.

Bottom: To light the Sabbath candles in the home at sundown on Friday and to pronounce the blessing over the flickering flame is the duty and the privilege of the housewife. An allegorical parallel between the flickering human soul and the Sabbath spirit which enters the home is implicit in this symbolic rite.

Top: Merrymaking through dance and song has, in the course of time, been enriched with new varieties of Jewish folk-dances and lively melodies. Graceful indoor group dances accompanied by singing, and vigorous and enthusiastic Palestinian dances marked by spirited steps and rounds are popular with the young people.

Bottom: Lessons in dancing and singing, expressions of Jewish life from Biblical times, are in great favor with the girls. Rhythmic movements suggestive of deep emotional experiences were once and still are today performed at religious festivals, family affairs, and weddings.

115

Dramatic interpretations of Biblical incidents are year-round activities which have a strong and lasting appeal. Pertinently underscoring the tenets of justice, honesty, respect for one's fellow men, kindness, exemplary family life, and the other ethical teachings of Judaism, these plays are performed by the children for their own edification and for the enjoyment of their parents. Passionately involved in dramatics, the youngsters put on costumes, prepare sets and props, study their parts as leading characters and supporting cast, and rehearse for the performance. Stories appropriate to the festivals are brought to the stage, including themes from the lives of the earliest nomadic ancestors and those grounded in Jewish folklore.

Top: Among the numerous plays is one concerning Joseph and his jealous brothers, who sold him into slavery in Egypt. Though spoiled by the privileges he succeeded in earning for himself at the court of the Pharaoh, Joseph acquired the virtue of forgiveness and generously helped his brothers, who had committed a crime against him.

Left: The Purim play and the carnival provide a thrill to which children look forward as the jolliest of all holidays. The Purim celebration connotes unshaken confidence in the triumph of justice over evil. The story of Esther, the proverbial maiden of rare beauty and staunch loyalty, of the steadfast Mordecai who clung to his Jewish beliefs in a foreign land, and of the ruthless Haman who schemed for the extermination of the Jews in Persia is read at the synagogue. Esther turns away from the wicked Haman as all Jews do from every Haman, who symbolizes their would-be destroyers.

The revelation on Mount Sinai takes dramatic form when the giving of the Law through Moses some 3300 years ago is re-enacted on Shavuoth, the Feast of the First Fruits. It is an occasion of praise and thankfulness for the many gifts received from the Almighty, especially for the greatest of all, God's covenant with Israel granting to His people the Torah with the Ten Commandments. Intended for every person and all nations, the Decalogue is an expression of man's striving for perfection. These basic teachings of Judaism have acquired universal acceptance, having become the spiritual possession of the entire Western Civilization.

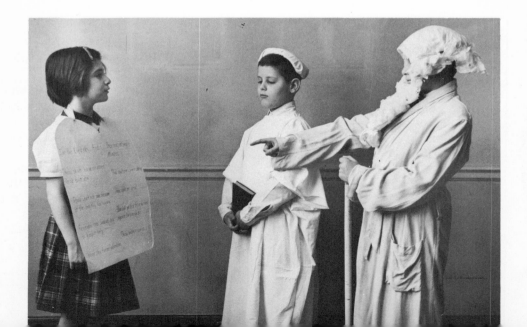

The inspired prophets of old who preached to the Jewish people at the village gates and on street corners were dedicated religious leaders, statesmen, and educators. Their ringing orations and eloquent writings are immortalized in the Holy Scriptures. The words of the prophets, many of them among the most exalted passages of the Hebrew Bible, are widely known and frequently quoted by communicants of other faiths. These men of vision and courage contributed eminently to the molding of Jewish thought and action by their utterances, which are of eternal validity.

The prophets spoke up forcefully against foreign idols and wickedness and exhorted the people to adhere to God and the Mosaic Law. They denounced oppression and social injustice and advocated human rights and social reform. With penetrating insight they foresaw doom and redemption, disaster and hope. They also gave a definite formulation to many fundamental teachings of the Jewish ethical code. In dramatizing the lessons of the prophets the youngsters make vivid such immortal pronouncements as Malachi's "Have we not all one father? Has not one God created us?" and Micah's "Only to do justly, and love mercy, and to walk humbly with thy God."

Congregational singing and the chanting of traditional melodies occupy a prominent place in Jewish worship. Some of the melodies chanted in the ancient Temple have survived orally from generation to generation and are still sung in synagogue services. The musical interpretation of popular prayers harks back as far as the fifth century. The children learn songs, including the moving Kol Nidre, chanted on the Day of Atonement since the eleventh century. They receive training in singing the traditionally established melodies as well as pieces of choral music.

The language of the Bible is one of the bonds that unite Jews throughout the world. In the synagogue the Holy Scriptures have been read in the original Hebrew ever since the time they were written. Though for almost twenty centuries the tongue of the ancestors was not used in everyday speech, it remained very much alive in the synagogues and schools. Pupils of the Religious Schools undertake the study of Hebrew. Later they will realize that they are better able to grasp the profound thoughts of the Bible and the beautiful stanzas of the Hebrew prayers and songs.

The little tots begin to learn the Aleph Beth, the Hebrew alphabet, and the Hebrew symbols of speech sounds. Puzzled at first by the difference from their native English, the children soon make progress in acquiring a Hebrew vocabulary with the aid of letter cards. Called on, they quickly line up to form a newly-learned word: "Yisroel."

The first-grader benefits from patient assistance in the proper reading of Hebrew lines from right to left and in the correct pronunciation of the words.

The children enlarge their vocabulary by acting out words and pronouncing them in Hebrew. With pleasure they dramatize the most frequently recurring words and read the cards which show pictures of objects and name them as well. The lively activity, combining body motion and the pronunciation of the words out loud, greatly helps the beginner to memorize a word like "bird."

Once in command of several words, the children concentrate on vocabulary practice. One youngster writes words on the board while others illustrate their meaning.

During the course of study the essentials of Hebrew grammar and sentence structure are introduced. In due time the students learn to build complete sentences and to speak them fluently. Thus the foundations for simple conversations are laid.

In the advanced grades the pupils develop fluency in reading selections from the prayer book. They also acquire the ability to transcribe text into script with grammatical accuracy, such as, "Thou shalt love the Lord thy God with all thy heart. . . ."

Prayers, blessings, and hymns, destined to remain with the youngsters throughout their life, are committed to memory from reading charts. The children learn to recite them by heart and to chant them in the traditional manner: "They that keep the Sabbath and call it a delight, shall rejoice in Thy kingdom...."

The broadened knowledge of Hebrew opens up new horizons. Mastery of the holy tongue facilitates access to the Talmud, the Mishnah, and the Gemara, without resort to translations. It enables the students to explore the vast spiritual treasures of the Hebrew classics.

The education of the young people for worship brings to them the uplifting personal experience of prayer. Intelligent and direct participation in Divine Service makes the children aware of God's claim upon them and calls forth their response to common worship. They become familiar with the liturgical practices of the Sabbath and the holidays, the prayers and songs for each occasion, and with the Torah ceremonials.

Top: Tradition encourages public prayer when a Minyan is assembled. Ten men, including boys over thirteen years of age, constitute the quorum that is needed for public worship. The Junior Congregation meets for the morning Minyan service, starting its day with prayer. In conformity with tradition, all worshippers wear the Tallit and put on the Tefillin.

Bottom: Strongly drawn by synagogical melodies, members of the cantors' group practice the musical part of the service. Training their voices, they learn to sing the Hebrew tunes and lead the congregation in chanting of prayers and singing hymns.

Top: Synagogues endeavor to establish their own libraries, well supplied with books and magazines for the pupils. The objective of Jewish education stems from the religious ideal of attaining perfection through study, knowledge, and wisdom. In discharging this duty the synagogue libraries are eager to provide young and old with worthwhile literature of interest to Jews. Teachers and students discuss and review books, and library sessions are designed to stimulate the children's affection for good books.

Left: The curiosity of young minds derives satisfaction from the books available at the Religious School's reading and lending library. The selections at their disposal aid them in developing a love for Jewish books and the habit of reading books.

The Judaica Shop, operated by the Sisterhood, directs attention to recent publications. From the shop new books and attractive ceremonial objects find their way into Jewish homes. During the Hanukah season, when customarily books are given as presents, valuable advice and guidance is offered through the annual Jewish Book Month celebration that is held about that time.

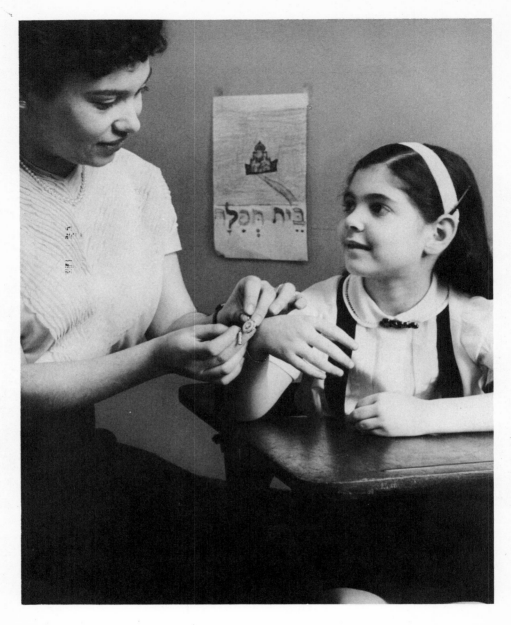

Religious instruction assumes a decisive role in molding the spiritual stature of the growing youth. In the classroom, at celebrations, in plays and school-wide activities the children find the spiritual nourishment their hearts and souls desire. Happy with their teachers and with one another, the pupils joyfully accept the little tokens they receive on birthdays and for work well done—a book, a tie-clip or bracelet with the Star of David.

CHAPTER SIX

COMING

OF

AGE

"The end of the matter, all having been heard; fear God,
and keep His commandments; for this is the whole man."

(*Ecclesiastes* 12:13)

The beginning of a boy's religious responsibilities marks a turning point in his life, a personal event that is publicly celebrated at the synagogue by the Bar Mitzvah ritual. Having been prepared for religious maturity through instruction, at thirteen he becomes a Man of Duty, a Son of the Commandment. The youth's initiation into religious duties must be preceded by study of the Law and understanding of Jewish living according to the Hebrew precept. It is expected of the Bar Mitzvah boy that he be able to read the Torah and to know the age-old customs when the privilege is given him to participate in the services.

Before his induction the Bar Mitzvah boy receives his own Tallit and Tefillin and learns to use them in the traditional way. Aware of the profound meaning of the phylacteries, he fastens one box to the left arm near his heart and places the other box on his forehead close to the intellect. This ancient symbolic act teaches him to commit his heart and his mind to the precepts of the ancestral faith as it is epitomized in the Biblical verses written on parchment and enclosed in the boxes.

On the first Sabbath of his fourteenth year the Bar Mitzvah boy is called up in the synagogue to read the Torah. This solemn act signifies the fact that henceforth he is to be regarded as a full member in the fold of Israel, having taken upon himself the religious obligations handed down from the fathers. By now he knows what the Torah means to him, to his fellow men, and to humanity as a whole. Counted as a grownup in religious matters, any time the Sacred Scroll is taken from the Ark he may receive the honor of carrying the Torah, of reading from it, of uncovering it or mantling it again.

The Bar Mitzvah boy reads the weekly portion from the Torah and chants the Haftorah, the lessons of the Prophets. Judaism makes it mandatory for every Jew from early childhood to read the Book of the Law and to gain a personal access to God through the Torah. He is now admitted to the Bar Mitzvah test in the presence of the whole congregation. The study of the Torah stands as a pillar of Jewish life. From the very beginning it promoted understanding of the Word of God and the spread of general education.

Following his reading, the Bar Mitzvah boy proceeds to the Ark. Facing the Torah, he makes his own pledge of loyalty to his faith and declares his desire to live a righteous life. Father and grandfather stand close to the heir of their faith in the new generation, while the rabbi invokes his blessing: "In the name of the Lord, our God, I invoke upon you the hallowed three-fold blessing with the prayer that you in turn may so live as to become a three-fold blessing to your faith, your country, your fellowmen. May the Lord bless you and keep you; may the Lord let His countenance shine upon you and be gracious unto you; may the Lord lift up His countenance upon you and give you peace. Amen."

A solemn and inspiring ceremony takes place in Reform and many Conservative synagogues on Shavuoth, the festival that commemorates the Giving of the Law. Young people of fifteen and sixteen form a processional to the synagogue to be confirmed before the entire congregation. The stately Confirmation Ceremony symbolically revives the event of the Sinai Covenant. It affords the occasion for the confirmants publicly to pledge themselves to the Mosaic faith, and for all the people present at the synagogue to reavow their allegiance to Jewish ideals.

דרשו יי בהמצאו קראהו בהיותו קרוב

Boys as well as girls solemnly affirm their resolve to become loyal members of the Jewish community and responsible citizens of the country. On this festive day the confirmants, like the Israelites on Mt. Sinai, accept God's Law, and each makes his or her own Declaration of Faith. Like the ancestors who brought offerings to the Temple, they place flowers of faith and dedication on the Ark of the synagogue. The rabbi, having solemnized their inauguration with his blessing, presents to each a Bible in the name of the congregation.

The confirmants are graduates of the confirmation class, where they received intensive instruction from the rabbi and the teachers of the Religious School. Their preparation reaches its climax at the confirmation ceremony marking their assumption of all the duties of mature Jews. The Bar Mitzvah and the Confirmation are occasions of joyful celebration at home, with family reunions and visits from friends, who offer gifts to the new full-fledged members of the Jewish community. The departure from childhood and the embarkation toward responsible adulthood is a crucial station in life emphatically pointed up by Jewish tradition. The solemn exercises held at the synagogue stand out as an event to be long remembered by the young people and by their parents as well.

The individual Bar Mitzvah and the group Confirmation designate the time when the young people take on the personal obligation of translating into deeds for themselves the teachings of Judaism. Both these rituals mean not the end of studies but their continuation on an advanced plane. Admonished by the Hebraic tradition, the synagogue's educational program for adults is bound to maintain the continuity of Jewish studies. Knowledge and understanding of the Jewish faith are pursued at the synagogue by various study groups, who learn the Torah, the Talmud, Hebrew language and literature, Jewish history and culture on a higher level. We see a group of young men and women equipping themselves with greater knowledge for helping to teach the young ones at the Religious School from which they have recently graduated.

CHAPTER SEVEN

THE RABBI

AND

HIS FLOCK

"For the priest's lips should keep knowledge,
And they should seek the law at his mouth."

(*Malachi* 2:7)

IN MEMORY OF JULIUS BRODY

Because "he is the messenger of the Lord of hosts," the rabbi is first and above all, a teacher of religion, as his title indicates. He occupies the pulpit as the expounder of Judaism and preacher to his people. The rabbi is the spiritual leader of the congregation and the community holds him in respect because of his dedication and his personal qualities. He guides the congregation in worship and furthers the religious life of the community. The spiritual successor of the Hebrew priests and prophets, the rabbi's function today has grown far beyond the confines of the Sanctuary.

In the service of his people, the rabbi discharges a crowded calendar of duties. In the administration of his office his secretary and aides assist him to keep in touch with the members of their families, and to oversee the smooth running of the religious, educational, and social affairs of the synagogue. Although the secular functions in Jewish congregations are delegated to individual members and groups of congregants, the rabbi shares in the responsibility for all activities taking place in his synagogue. More often than not, he is burdened with details, and the demands on him are very heavy: he devotes himself to matters pertaining to worship and to pastoral ministration, and to these are added obligations of organizational and executive work.

The rabbi teaches the will of God. As the spokesman for God and as a man of learning he enjoys authority among the Jewish people. Trained in Jewish law and tradition, he perpetuates religious values in modern life, affecting the thinking and feeling of old and young alike. In his study the rabbi advises his congregants on family problems, parents on the education of children, young couples on marriage, and to the happy and the troubled he offers the answers of the Jewish faith. In counseling individuals and in delivering his message from the pulpit, the rabbi faces up to the issues of our complex age. Absorbed in constant study, week in and week out he prepares his sermons for the Sabbath and the festivals, and transmits divine instruction in terms of the day at hand.

The rabbi gives personal attention to the children's religious training and it is part of his office to supervise the Religious School in his congregation. He cooperates with the Religious School Committee and the educational director in formulating school policy and developing the program of study. The principal and a staff of competent teachers, maintaining professional standards, engage in the administration and execution of the school program. At the opening of the school year and on special occasions the rabbi addresses the children; he visits them in the classrooms and evinces appreciation of their achievements. At the closing exercises he speaks to the assembly of young people and makes awards to those with outstanding scholastic records.

Historically a place of study and charitable work, the synagogue lives up to its great tradition by maintaining facilities through which members may seek knowledge and volunteer with their services for the common good. Stressing these aims, one of the rabbis, in large congregations, assumes charge of the extensive educational program and social activities. Both are separately carried forward for the junior groups and the adults. Stimulating the youth to take an interest in their synagogue and in the affairs of the larger Jewish community, the rabbi conducts courses, lectures to groups, and leads discussions, helping his listeners to find their way as Jews and as good citizens.

While the young are introduced to the fundamentals of Judaism, the adults are drawn together in the study of works from the rich collections of the writings and commentaries produced by the sages and scholars. The rabbi presides over the sessions of the Talmud study group, exploring the great encyclopedia of Jewish lore and life with those who are versed in the Hebraic literature. The Law given to Moses and written in the Torah was explained and commented on by rabbis and scholars of later ages. The Talmud became dear to the people as standard study. With respect and affection, advanced study groups delve into the expositions and polemics of the most brilliant minds who have investigated and amplified Holy Writ through their life-long studies.

The unbroken continuity of teaching and learning runs through Jewish history; it was this that sustained the old truth of an old faith from generation to generation. Scholarly rabbis, elucidating sacred doctrines, have been in the past and are today engaged in the informal instruction of future rabbis and in lecturing at schools of higher learning. Authorities in Hebraic knowledge, they eloquently formulate Jewish thought in papers and books. In earlier days the rabbi was primarily a student of the Law, whose chief function was to pass judgment on ritual and communal matters and resolve disputes among Jews. But the requirements of the modern synagogue place upon him many other duties. To meet these demands his knowledge of Jewish lore is supplemented with a broad secular training, and his preparation for the rabbinate is brought to completion with college degrees and ordination in a rabbinical seminary.

The Jewish concept of family life ascribes supreme importance to a harmonious and stable marriage and to the responsible rearing of children. The rabbi solemnizes the great moment when the bride and the groom are joined in wedlock. He reminds the young couple of Jewish family ethics revealed in the Law, of companionship, love, and consecration to each other. The bride and the groom stand side by side before the rabbi under the Chupah, the wedding canopy symbolic of the common roof that binds them together and to Israel. The hallowed event is sanctified by the recital of benedictions and the observance of ancient customs with deep religious meaning. The bride and the groom take a sip of wine from the common cup, and the groom gives the ring to his bride. Then he stamps on a glass, breaking it into splinters, whereupon the guests extend the traditional Mazel Tov, their good wishes for the start of a successful marriage.

The rabbi, devoted to his flock, ministers to the members of his congregation in hours of joy as well as at times when suffering visits them. He calls at the homes of sick congregants, encouraging the convalescents to bear their idleness until they can carry on with renewed health. He is in attendance at the nearby hospitals and homes for the aged, bringing solace and spiritual strength to the afflicted and the shut-in. The rabbi prays with them and helps to restore their hopes. This he does, too, on his visit to correctional institutions. His presence there furthers the rehabilitation of the inmates, inspiring them with confidence in society and interest in a respectable life.

Rabbis give of their time to Jewish communal undertakings, fostering unity and cooperation among their congregations. The Orthodox, Conservative, and Reform branches have their national, regional and local organizations for the benefit of their affiliated synagogues. Rabbis work together in rabbinical, and laymen in lay units, and leaders of both meet, under the auspices of the Synagogue Council of America, representing American Jewry as a whole on major moral, social and religious issues. On the local level the boards or councils, composed of Orthodox, Conservative, and Reform rabbis, exchange views and map programs for ministering to Jewish needs and for upholding in their community the sacred traditions of the synagogue.

The rabbi's voice reaches beyond his pulpit and reverberates in the larger community when he participates in communal causes and civic ceremonies. Frequently invited to address general audiences, patriotic and interfaith gatherings, he acquaints them with Jewish principles and their fulfillment in social and cultural life. In small towns and in the great centers of the United States, the rabbi participates in community projects and takes a leading part in civic affairs, coping with the challenging problems of everyday life. Speaking over the radio and on television, rabbis attain wide recognition for their searching orations, ministering to the soul and urging civic betterment.

In time of peace and in time of war, the rabbi dons the uniform and serves the needs of men in the military forces. From isolated outposts in the Arctic to scattered installations in Asia and Africa, in posts and hospitals throughout Europe and America, the Jewish chaplain cares for the morale and welfare of the Jewish personnel, providing religious services and pastoral guidance.

Through his personal contact, the rabbi is the symbol of home and representative of the Jewish community for thousands of soldiers, sailors, and airmen. He discusses their problems with them, helps in holiday observances, carries out educational programs, and holds Torah Convocations. The rabbi's activities in uniform include such gratefully received services as the distribution of gift packages, prayer books, Jewish literature, Sabbath and Yahrzeit candles, and the furnishing of food—blintzes, fish, matzoth, and sacramental wine—for the celebration of the holidays.

Through the whole cycle of human life the rabbi stands by his flock, from the coming into the world to the return to dust. He attends his congregants, the living and the dead, with the hallowed rituals of the Jewish faith. He comforts the mourners, officiates at the interment, and after a year has passed and the gravestone has been set, he unveils it and leads in prayer at the dedication ceremony. On occasions of sorrow and of happiness the rabbi spares no effort to share with his people the spiritual observances Judaism has instituted for the fateful junctures in man's journey on earth.

CHAPTER EIGHT

THE LAYMEN AND THEIR CONGREGATION

"Thy testimonies have I taken as a heritage for ever; For they are the rejoicing of my heart."
(*Psalm* 119:111)

Laymen, steeped in the Jewish tradition, unselfishly volunteer their services to aid their congregation in achieving the goal of a flourishing religious home. They heed the summons for the erection of a new synagogue or the expansion of its facilities. The same age-old custom has prevailed since the days of Moses, when he requested the people to make contributions in kind and in valuable objects to the building of the Sanctuary in the wilderness. The ancient Hebrews brought their free-will offerings for the maintenance of the Sanctuary, and Jews of today discharge their obligations through their monetary gifts.

The Jewish way of life is rooted in the synagogue and tied to the measure of devotion the congregants extend to it. It is the membership of the congregation that advances the cause of the synagogue and bears the responsibility of meeting its material needs. From the day the congregation is established, it relies on the contributions of its members to defray its expenses. As the Biblical parable has it, the strength and influence of Jewish knowledge is like a tree, branching out in all directions. Frequent references are made in Hebrew writings to the Torah as being a "tree of life" to them who hold fast to this repository of wisdom. As guardians of the Torah and sponsors of the synagogue, Jews make substantial donations in support of their faith. Evidencing their devotion to the house of God, the congregants inscribe memorable events in their lives on the synagogue's "Tree of Life" or Happy Events Tablet and in memorial books.

Each congregation stands by itself as a voluntary association, putting Jewish teachings into effect and serving the community. Independent and free of control by any compulsive authority, the Torah and Jewish tradition motivate the faithful as they cope with the practical problems of the congregation. The laymen's role in Jewish life and in the affairs of the synagogue is underscored by the democratic spirit of Judaism. All officers are elected at the annual membership meeting from among the constituency. They constitute the governing body in charge of the congregation's management and policy. Through the representative procedure, the actual government of the synagogue is vested in the president, the vice-president, the treasurer, the secretary, the trustees, and the members of the committees. They all are voluntary lay workers and discharge manifold duties, whereas the general direction and control of the congregation and its institutions are placed in the hands of the board of trustees. The officers and members of the various standing committees, such as finance, religious school, building, ritual, cemetery, and membership, meet regularly, and each of them performs specific functions defined in the By-Laws of the congregation.

The officers make it their business to provide, through careful and efficient administration, adequate facilities for religious, educational, welfare, and communal activities. They are occupied with budget planning and balancing, with membership dues and sources of income, with fundraising and the enlistment of voluntary workers, and with the many other details that contribute to the successful operation of the congregation. The building has to be maintained in good condition, the employees' salaries and daily expenses paid, all activities planned in advance and then properly executed. The rabbi's advice on the drawing up of plans is often sought by the officers, and they labor together on many projects. The rabbi's zeal and determination to keep high the synagogue's religious life and community services brings about close cooperation between him and all the officers and every working unit.

Judaism does not merely profess beliefs, but makes them vital through action that follows its ideals. The synagogue is a focal point of the Jewish way of living, giving wide expression to it in spirit and in deeds. A variety of auxiliaries, designed for every member of the family, enlist talents and energies to further the cause of the synagogue and the whole community. Men, women, and young people form their own units and carry out religious programs, cultural projects, and social work. Men band together in the Brotherhood or the Men's Club, women in the Sisterhood or the Women's Guild, and a number of other affiliated groups advance and strengthen the synagogue through their planned activities. Separately or jointly, each of them holds frequent meetings and social gatherings.

Under the guidance of its president the Men's Club offers a series of events, lectures by noted speakers, forums with debates, recreation with entertainment. The wholesome environment of the Community House binds the members in congenial companionship. Otherwise busy family heads appreciate the opportunity of spending some hours together in diversions from their daily pursuits. The Men's Club arranges informal affairs, such as father-and-son dinners, outings and picnics, games or parties to attend sports events. Many members of the Men's Club are busy with general congregational matters, devoting their spare time to duties as functionaries. They assist officers, provide workers for communal undertakings, fund-raising and membership campaigns, and make their purses available for good purposes.

Quick in initiative and far-reaching in accomplishments is the Sisterhood with its broad program of religious and cultural activities, and social services. When effort, time, and willing hands are needed, the ladies of the Sisterhood efficiently play their parts in congregational projects. They enhance them with numerous additions of their own, frequently marked by the feminine touch. Largely mothers and homemakers, with keen understanding for practical solutions, ingenuity inspires the Sisterhood in demonstrating religious concern in practical ways. The range of their services extends from intimate tea parties in their homes, whose proceeds may go for purchasing some furniture for the congregation, to fund soliciting for the large-scale drives set by the national organizations of Jewish philanthropies. The members convene and hear reports, discuss and adopt plans, explore ways and means, and follow the leadership of the Sisterhood's president and her helpers.

The patronesses of many events are the busy bees of the congregation, prepared to work throughout the year for the benefit of the synagogue, the Jewish community, and for society as a whole. The Sisterhood is particularly attracted to the fields of education, benevolent work, and contributions to congregational life in various forms. In fulfillment of one of the fundamental Jewish duties, women dedicate themselves to the never completed task of helping others. The energy they pour into personal services, their proficiency in reaching religious goals, account for the prominent role that Jewish women play in American Jewish life. The variety of the women's interests led to the formation of numerous and diverse Sisterhood activities. Whether it is a hand that has to be given in the kitchen of the Community Center or leadership that must be assumed for time-consuming enterprises, the ladies of the Sisterhood join hands to do the best they can. Seeking no rewards, they are content with the commendation of their fellow workers and a small gift as a token of appreciation for meritorious services.

מרבה צדקה
מרבה שלום
United Jewish Appeal
Federation of Jewish Charities
Hadassah
Hebrew Immigrant Aid Society
Jewish National Fund

Judaism commands the performance of Mitzvah, various acts that are helpful to religion, fellow Jews, and the community. The synagogue gives impulse to the Mitzvah of Tzedakah, too. A high place in the order of ethical virtues is accorded to Tzedakah, which means righteousness, the righteous giving in behalf of justice. By precept and by practice Tzedakah implies a charitable self-taxation for the purpose of allocating a just share of one's fortune for those in need. Adults and young people alike are charged with this obligation. In the Religious School and in youth societies children drop their money regularly into Tzedakah-boxes and leave charity envelopes containing donations. Boys and girls contribute to the Keren Ami, or Fund of My People; they collect for welfare organizations, and support particular causes of their choice.

Challenged by the physical and spiritual tribulations of others, young folks become aware of the financial needs that confront Jewish welfare agencies. American Jewry has developed efficient national organizations, which face and attack social and welfare problems. These gather funds to carry out the collective responsibilities of the Jewish community. The

Federations of Jewish Philanthropies care for many hundreds of affiliated agencies throughout the United States, supporting institutions for the poor, the sick, the handicapped, the orphaned and the aged, and those concerned with child care and family services. The United Jewish Appeal helps distressed Jews in all areas of the world, rehabilitating and resettling them with the funds it receives. Zionist groups concentrate on relief to Jews in Israel, on the construction of educational and cultural institutions, which foster the aspiring civilization of the restored homeland.

At the conclusion of the juniors' charity campaign, votes are taken on the allotments to be made to each of the beneficiaries selected. The young people carry out a number of other projects, too, such as rounds from house to house to collect clothing, shoes, and food for the needy.

The teen-agers go into action, pooling their efforts in their own particular ways. The will to be of service to others originates activities imbued with the genuine feeling of charity. The synagogue's senior high school group, divided into squads, sets out to do chores: house cleaning, window and car washing, gardening, and baby sitting. From the considerable sums they have earned, the boys and girls make donations to various agencies. Prompted by the Community Workday, they present their check in the name of the synagogue to the Interfaith Youth Council for its community projects.

The young folks of the congregation often stage amateur shows and sponsor social evenings with dancing. Their enthusiasm never fails to fill the auditorium of the Community House with friends and relatives. Full of expectation, they count the box-office receipts and turn them over to worthy causes.

The educational programs of the Sisterhood attract large audiences of members and friends. Such timely topics as family life, children's education, new books, race relations and interdenominational cooperation, housing and homemaking, are discussed by experts to the profit and pleasure of all those present. Here, for instance, the Sisterhood attends a lecture-demonstration on flowers and floral arrangements, with instructions for the traditional display on Jewish festivals and holidays. The Sisterhood nurtures community spirit and friendly relations in the congregational family. It sponsors theater and concert benefits, community dinners, fashion revues, and garden parties. These as well as bazaars, auctions, and rummage sales produce funds which are channeled to meet widespread needs.

The sale of useful articles that are displayed on tables, and of Jewish art objects, books, and records at the Judaica Shop of the Community Center, is as much a part of fund-raising for charity as card parties and raffles. Some of the merchandise on sale and the prizes for the drawing are donated by members and good neighbors. Nevertheless, the running of such affairs calls for work and more work in order to assure success.

Thousands of hands give hundreds of thousands of hours every year to the various circles of the Sisterhoods, promoting the purposes of agencies engaged in the sacred work of healing and mercy. In the workrooms of the Community House women perform services for unknown persons but for well-known aims. With the cooperation of national organizations, streams of gifts flow out to our soldiers, holiday packages and bags with articles that bring a little comfort to them. Packed and shipped by the ladies of the Sisterhoods, they carry warmth and affection to the men in uniform. The ways of charitable work may have changed since Biblical times, but it is still at its best when Jewish women join their skills to clothe the naked and brighten those who feel they are forgotten. As the bundles of garments multiply in the sewing rooms, the morale of the needy rises at home and overseas.

Congregational groups join in community undertakings with other synagogues and with churchwomen of other faiths to carry out social and humanitarian plans. A number of ladies prepare surgical dressings for hospitals or do service with the Red Cross or give blood to the blood bank, while others represent the synagogue in neighborhood and community agencies. Benevolent groups raise money for some favored institutions, granting rabbinical scholarships, beautifying the synagogue, or helping girls to a happy marriage and to the establishment of their families. But whatever may be the goals they set for themselves, the ultimate purpose is to make the religious vision of the Mitzvah a reality. The acceptance of the obligation to perform deeds of love, perseverance in the Mitzvah throughout Jewish history, has ever upheld the reputation of Jewish generosity.

Acts of kindness are incumbent upon every Jew. Ever thoughtful of fellow members, the visiting committee of the Sisterhood extends felicitations to young mothers and welcomes new arrivals. Representatives of the Sisterhood and of the Men's Club alike pay visits to friends on appropriate occasions. Sharing joy when happy events knock at the door, and comforting the sick and the bereaved are among the practices Jews learn from their Bible.

CHAPTER NINE

THE SYNAGOGUE

COMMUNITY

CENTER

"Behold, how good and how pleasant it is
For brethren to dwell together in unity!"
(*Psalm* 133:1)

The American synagogue is bound to revive Jewish community life effectively and bring about sociability and friendly relationships among its members. The form and ways of modern life have broken into all group associations, including the synagogue-centered community. The Community Center is an open house seven days a week, offering a place for the cultivation of friendships and warm fellowship. The individual American Jew identifies himself with every phase of the national, cultural, and economic life. At the same time, he lives up to his religion and to American democracy, both of which are equally concerned with the happiness of every individual and with the well-being of all the people. The Community Center invites participation in worth-while recreation and social get-togethers. Its varied programs are designed to enrich everyday life through informal education and leisure-time activities, through giving and receiving fellowship. The Community Center provides an intimate home for an intensive community life, ranging from social hours with refreshments to gala dinners, from reading in the library to dance parties.

The social hall of the Community House takes on color and a festive air when numerous distinguished guests join with the congregational family to honor outstanding members at testimonial dinners. On such memorable occasions the congregation tenders citations and tokens of appreciation to the guest of honor, and leaders from every walk of life and from all religious denominations come to deliver addresses. Among those to whom warm tribute is paid is the rabbi: on his anniversary, his flock and the whole community heap honors on him, who has endeared himself to them during a long and devoted ministry.

The Men's Club and other auxiliaries of the congregation tender their respects to their fellows who have earned their esteem for achievements as Jews and as citizens. The meeting rooms at the Community House are a scene of gladness as well-wishing friends, the rabbi, and the synagogue officers salute celebrated members.

The men's breakfast club on Sunday morning, the ladies' tea parties in the afternoon, and the hours set aside for games for the young folks throughout the week are among the attractions in a lighter vein. However, the whole community, both parents and children, join in congregational festivities, like the Purim Carnival, the Simchath Torah, and the Hanukah Party.

The Community Center's library and reading room assume the significant function of making available works of Jewish literature, the masterpieces of the past and new publications as well. Through the purchase of current books, the synagogue libraries help to stimulate contemporary Jewish literature. The people of the Book produced and assimilated outstanding literary creations long before the advent of the printing press. Many congregations are proud to possess revered works of Judaica in Hebrew and in other tongues. Eminent Jewish scholars, poets, and philosophers in olden days kept the light bright and achieved enduring fame. They can be found on the shelves or may be borrowed from the rabbi's study. In the company of modern authors such renowned names may be seen as Solomon Ibn Gabirol, Rashi, Judah Halevi, Abraham Ibn Ezra, Moses Maimonides, Joseph Caro, and many others.

The youth societies of the congregation satisfy the needs of their members with a choice of activities planned to suit the interests and the tastes of different age groups. Well-balanced projects unite young people in religious services and study groups, reaching also into the field of recreational activities. The year-round social affairs at the Community House confer on the young people the benefits of good companionship, and so does the common pursuit of favorite hobbies. Here is a group that organizes hikes, week-end excursions, and one-day trips including outdoor activities. Young men and women meet every Sunday morning in front of the synagogue and set forth to enjoy themselves in the fresh air with games, cameras, and radios.

In the intelligent building of any human resources, the training of the mind and physical fitness go hand in hand. Having attended their classes in religious instruction, the younger set takes over the gymnasium, playing ping pong, basketball, volley ball, and other games. In the evening the seniors take advantage of the facilities at the Community Center, doing gymnastics and playing ball.

Outward expressions of joy and of happiness have been traditional manifestations of Jewish life. Recreational events at the Community Center renew the geniality and cheerful dignity that tinged social gatherings in the Jewish past. The Bible and the Talmud relate that dances and music enhanced numerous occasions, and during the ages of hardship, both continued to gladden the heart when the people amused themselves in their leisure time. The Hebrew dances and songs of antiquity, frequently performed at religious and social festivities, survived for long periods. Yet in the dispersion the influence of the environment was felt in popular entertainment and new motifs colored the Jewish folk dances. Some of these old ones and new Palestinian dances crop up on joyous occasions; the march of time, however, did not stop at the doors of the ball rooms. Entertainments, featuring floor shows, dance contests, and games serve the common objectives of making friends and helping charitable causes. Whether one wins or loses, it is all good fun because in every case the proceeds go to charity.

181

Musical events at the Community House realize the aims of those who dedicate themselves to the performance of Hebraic music, past and present. Receptive audiences respond when programs are offered by the synagogue choir or the music groups of the congregation, and the auditorium resounds with melodies that reflect the Hebraic spirit and Hebrew musical idiom.

Members of the congregation and their children who are fond of singing and making music organize choral groups and orchestral ensembles. They perform for their own pleasure and for that of their fellow congregants. Music was popular among the ancient Hebrews, and ever since it has figured prominently in divine services. The singing by the great choruses in the Temple of Jerusalem, the singers and musicians at the harvest and national celebrations, initiated a musical tradition that Jews have carried with them to the many countries where they have made their homes. Ancient tunes show up in the liturgical music, and they reappear also in the popular melodies evoked by the Jewish existence in the countries of Europe and in the remote areas of the Orient. Rich and colorful in religious themes and folk songs is the imposing storehouse of Jewish music. In love songs, lullabies, and ballads, gay wedding songs and musical poetry of deep melancholy, the emotions of the soul well up to the lips. The music of the Bible and of the ghetto, Ashkenazic, Hassidic, Sephardic, and Oriental tunes are in the repertory of these ambitious amateur groups. Bridging the gap between the ages, the interpreters of the old also render selections from the revitalized musical culture of Israel and from modern Jewish compositions of American artists.

At the Jewish Community House people are also served who are not members of the congregation, discharging the function of a neighborhood center for the larger community. It extends hospitality to civic and educational organizations, placing at their disposal rooms for meetings and activities. Sectarian associations, like the Jewish War Veterans and fraternal orders, and a score of nonsectarian cultural and social groups, such as literary and philatelic clubs, find accommodation there.

Boy Scout and Girl Scout troops are among the permanent guests at the Community Center, and they feel at home in its quarters. In spiritual kinship with Jewish tenets, they take the Scout Oath and pledge adherence to the Scout Law: "A Scout is reverent. He is reverent toward God. He is faithful in his religious duties and respects the convictions of others in matters of custom and religion." In recognition of the importance of religious training and the responsibility of the home and the synagogue for it, the Ner Tamid Scout Award is given to Jewish Scouts who have prepared themselves, through successful Jewish studies, to put into practice the ideals of the Scout pledge. Whatever the units to which the youngsters belong, they all carry on the general scouting program and proudly wear the blue-and-white-ribboned Ner Tamid Medal together with the other badges. Reminding the boys of Israel's eternal zeal in serving God, the rabbi, in a solemn ceremony, pins on the Scout the Eternal Light Medal on which is engraved the Perpetual Lamp that burns in the synagogue.

Interfaith lectures and exhibits for fellow citizens of other faiths disseminate understanding of Judaism and awareness of the spiritual heritage that is common to all religious denominations in America. The synagogue opens its doors to church groups and to everyone who seeks knowledge of the ancient Hebrews and of their contemporary descendants. Christian laymen and children's groups, Sunday school teachers and ministers tour the synagogues and receive information on the Jewish religion. With some of what they see and hear, they are acquainted from their own Bible which also contains to a large extent the Jewish Bible. Here we see a scholarly lecture taking place before a distinguished audience of Christian clergymen. Outstanding authorities offer insight into Jewish life and thought, and discussions follow in an atmosphere of ministerial fellowship.

The Christian clergymen view the Sanctuary and acquaint themselves with its symbols and ceremonial practices. The Torah, well-spring
of all Western religions, here shown in its original Hebrew form, pro-
vokes a great many questions. Authentic facts on the Holy Scroll and
religious utensils enlighten the visitors. Hebrew sages stressed that many
Torahs spread more and more knowledge to more and more people, and
since time immemorial synagogues have possessed several Scrolls for study.
To donate a Torah and religious vessels to the house of God is regarded
as one of the most honorable of deeds. Each Scroll is a parchment roll
containing text, carefully written by hand, of the Pentateuch, the Five
Books of Moses. This is the first of the three parts of the Jewish Bible
and the primary source of the Jewish religion. The gold and silver ornaments symbolize the reverence and esteem in which the Sacred Law is
held. The ancient custom of reading the Torah in weekly portions is well
appreciated by the visitors, for the reading of the Sunday lesson from their
Bible manifests the common love for the Word of God felt by each faith.

The threefold mission of the synagogue — the worship of God, man's spiritual growth, and the practical living of religion — flows from the depths of Judaism. The Judaic concept of the fatherhood of God and the brotherhood of man had its origin in the synagogue, which, for millennia pioneered in its dissemination.

To build religion, understanding, and good will among all the people, from Central Synagogue in New York City the Message of Israel goes out over the air and is heard by listeners throughout the United States and overseas.

The synagogue and other Jewish institutions expound the teachings of Judaism over radio and television to a vast congregation. Devotional themes and Biblical narratives, brought into the homes of millions of Americans, lift the spirit and kindle the hope of coreligionists and fellow-citizens of every creed.

188

Lessons from Holy Writ and Jewish prayers ring out from the pulpit, and liturgical melodies float down from the choir loft. Noted rabbis preaching sermons advert to the spiritual resources of the Jewish faith and direct attention to the dangers of drifting away from religious truth and its knowledge. In the turmoil of life and in the tumultuous currents of onrushing events, the synagogue speaks as a guide on the road to divine fulfillment. The spokesmen of Judaism carry the ideals and traditions from the arsenal of the Jewish faith out into the world to edify and to instruct the multitude and to contribute to the advancement of the American way of life. The highest gifts Israel has given to eternity are to be shared by all the people: One God acknowledged by all men, and a united humanity striving to establish His Kingdom on earth.